100 Meals
for $5 or Less

100 Meals
for $5 or Less

Jennifer Maughan

GIBBS SMITH
TO ENRICH AND INSPIRE HUMANKIND
Salt Lake City | Charleston | Santa Fe | Santa Barbara

First Edition
09 10 11 12 13   5 4 3 2
Text © 2009 Jennifer Maughan

Published by
Gibbs Smith, Publisher
P.O. Box 667
Layton, Utah 84041

Orders: 1.800.835.4993
www.gibbs-smith.com

Designed by Natalie Peirce
Printed and bound in Canada

Library of Congress Cataloging-in-Publication Data

Maughan, Jennifer.
100 meals for $5 or less / Jennifer Maughan. — 1st ed.
        p. cm.
ISBN-13: 978-1-4236-0284-2
ISBN-10: 1-4236-0284-6
1. Low budget cookery. I. Title. II. Title: One hundred meals for five dollars or less.
TX652.M323 2009
641.5'52—dc22
                    2008030481

To Dad and Mom,

the grocery king and
the kitchen queen

Contents

Acknowledgements

Thank you to the staff at Gibbs Smith, especially to Michelle Witte, for believing in this project and working tirelessly with me to make it the best it can be.

Special thanks to my parents, Sheldon and Jane Kinsel, for providing such happy childhood memories around the dinner table and continuing to set the standard for us all.

Thanks to my sisters and brothers for various contributions of recipes, advice and encouragement. Also, thanks to my husband's family, who have also provided me with inspiration and aid.

My wonderful children, Abigail, William and Sarah, make the quest for delicious and healthy meals so worthwhile. Finally, I'm grateful for my husband, Jaceson, for his constant support and endless encouragement.

Introduction

Proven Money-Saving Methods

If you've picked up this book, you are someone who feels frustrated at how much things cost nowadays—clothing, cars, office supplies, utilities and more. All too often, it seems that there's never quite enough to cover all the bills and allow for the little extras that life throws at you—from emergency car repairs to school clothes for the kids. Even families who earn enough and live within their means encounter instances when a few hundred dollars extra would really come in handy, perhaps to put toward a family vacation, pay down credit card debts or contribute to a savings plan.

Short of getting a part-time job or asking the boss for a raise, it might seem like there's nothing much you can do to change things. While it's not too difficult to put off buying luxury items, there's no putting off the need to buy groceries and feed your family. However, many people are discovering that by cutting wasteful spending from their household food budget, they can make the dollars they do earn go further.

The time has come to take a good look at the money you spend on food. This book will give you tips and advice on how to trim the fat from your family's food budget—one of the few areas of spending you can actually control. Besides providing you with imaginative recipes made from low-cost ingredients, this book offers advice on budget-saving techniques such as menu planning, analyzing the psychology of shopping, the invaluable price list and more. In a few short weeks, you can develop some good shopping and cooking habits that will benefit yourself, your family and your wallet.

Cut Wasteful Spending

A recent study by the Bureau of Labor Statistics estimates that the average American family spends more than $8,000 per year on food. Compare that to other monthly expenses, and the grocery bill usually comes in as the second biggest after the mortgage or rent. With an average of $700 spent each month at the grocery store, the average family can really use some help. The good news is that the family's food budget is the best place to cut wasteful spending. You can't easily change your mortgage or car payment, but with some planning, determination and a positive attitude, you can trim your grocery bill, become a smarter shopper and still eat well. Imagine cutting your family grocery bill by a third or even half! Think of what you could do with a few hundred "extra" dollars a month. With smart meal planning and savvy shopping, you don't need to get another job—simply make your current income stretch a little further.

Imagine that trimming your food budget is a small part-time job. With a few hours of effort each week, you can save thousands of dollars each year, depending on how dedicated you want to be. The great news is that this is a part-time job that everyone can do—no experience needed. Even if you only apply half of the advice presented here, you'll notice a difference in how you cook, shop and save. Once you learn and practice these smart shopping and cooking techniques, it'll become second nature to you. Since grocery shop-ping and cooking meals for your family is something you have to do anyway, why not have a little fun, try some new cost-efficient recipes and save money at the same time?

Trial and Error

When my husband was in law school, we managed an apartment complex to make ends meet. We perfected the art of thrifty living; yet, as poor students, it grew increasingly frustrating to stare into the pantry at nothing but spaghetti ingredients. Sometimes we'd walk on the wild side and have tomato meat sauce rather than garden vegetable sauce. I was determined to see how I could improve the situation and serve different foods, instead of spaghetti.

I quizzed my parents, who raised seven (well-fed) kids, and got lots of good advice there. I scoured my cookbooks for recipes that were healthy and delicious yet didn't cost more than spaghetti ingredi-ents. Through trial and error and a little research, I was able to make it work. Slowly and surely, I figured out how to bargain shop and still create pleasing meals for my family.

As a result, we didn't have to face three years of spaghetti, nor did we break the bank.

Even now, with three kids, two pets, a mortgage and a job, I still enjoy managing the food budget to allow for fun extras. I take advantage of sales, bargains and quality discount stores. I love to challenge myself to come up with great meals that cost pennies. It's fun, it makes the paychecks go further, and I love the compliments my family gives me during a delicious meal.

Step By Step

Anyone interested in saving money should really learn the art of smart shopping and budget meal planning. These recipes are some of the best around and use ingredients that are frequently on sale or are generally some of the least expensive at regular price.

For those of you who have never thought about trimming your grocery budget, the steps are set up in a simple, straight-forward way. You can try a few to see how you and your family like them, and then try a few more. Quite soon, you'll be noticing some significant savings and the quality of your meals will increase. If you are an experienced budget shopper, there are plenty of things here for you to try that you've maybe never considered before. Instead of dining for months on spaghetti, try some of these tried-and-true methods to save more money on groceries.

Your new part-time job is to learn and apply the techniques in this book and mix them with a bit of your own common sense. Take the opportunity to make a change and then decide just how you're going to spend all the money you save. Join me in preparing low-cost meals and saving a few dollars. See what it feels like to find great recipes that your family asks for again and again. Experience the thrill of really seeing an impact in your budget. I know you can do it, so let's get started.

Chapter 1
Before You Shop

A workable food budget begins not with a skillet or a slow cooker, but with a sheet of paper and a pencil. When you can see numbers in black and white of how much you are actually spending on food, it may shock you. However, it is possible to lower the amount you spend on food without resorting to drastic measures, such as serving boxed macaroni and cheese five days a week. With strategic planning and flawless execution, you can still get good food for less than you're spending now.

Have a Plan

The truth is, the best way to blow your food budget is to go into it without a plan. I know we've all been there, staring into the freezer at the frozen chicken and glancing back into the nearly empty cupboard. After a few minutes, you sigh and dig out the take-out Chinese food menu. This scene can be avoided with about an hour or two of your time each week, by planning meals for each night and shopping accordingly.

Any book, article or Web site dealing with smart shopping will tell you that the worst thing you can do when going grocery shopping is to show up without a list. They also advise you to never, ever deviate from that list. What those well-meaning writers fail to tell you is how to come up with that list. In this section, we'll take it step by step, and soon you'll have all the information you need to begin.

Creating a shopping list is a mixture of detective work, creative cooking and puzzle-solving, but once you get the hang of it, you'll notice big savings on your grocery bill. You'll also notice that you're spending less on unhealthy, expensive fast food.

There are five important steps for creating a grocery-shopping list, and it doesn't include quickly writing down some jumbled notes in the parking lot just before entering the store. It doesn't mean rushing into the store just before dinner and throwing things into the cart. Rather, it is an intricate guide to that week's food specials combined with great recipes that complement each other. Finally, you must take into account what your family likes and dislikes and determine how all these factors merge together.

Step 1 What's on Sale?

The weekly fliers from the local grocery stores arrive in the mailbox or newspaper each week to tempt you to choose their store for all your shopping needs. Take advantage of these freebies and hold onto them until you're ready to make a weekly list. A little basket on a shelf, an old magazine rack or even a desk drawer will work nicely. Choose a time when you'll be uninterrupted for at least an hour, such as in the evenings after the kids are in bed. Grab the flyers, a paper and pencil and you're ready.

Smart spenders know that the key to the greatest savings depends on purchasing the best sale items listed in the weekly flyers. Combined with coupons, the food items can be purchased at greatly reduced prices. Even if you don't clip coupons, taking advantage of the weekly sales is a good habit.

Know that in the weeklies, the stores are going to promote "loss leaders," which are popular items that they are selling at cost or even less to get you into their store. They will be the very best deals around on those items, especially if you combine them with coupons. Most grocery stores cycle through sales about every ten to twelve weeks; that is, you'll see items like milk, soda, cheese and frozen vegetables crop up in cycles as the loss leaders. Once you get the hang of budget shopping, you can stock up on most of these items whenever they are on sale to last you through the entire cycle.

Note which items are on sale this week. Is it chicken? Sausage? Which store has the best ground beef prices? Scan the pages to see which primary meal items are on special. If chicken is on sale for a great price, but you don't see much mention of ground beef, then you'll know to plan at least three chicken meals this week, and use leftovers accordingly. Is asparagus in season? Use this sale to add that healthy vegetable into your diet over the next few days.

STORE NAME	ITEM	ITEM SIZE	COST
Grocery Joe's	Brand A bacon	12 ounces	$2.50
Grocery Joe's	House brand milk	1 gal.	$3.00 (2 for $6)
Shopper's Market	Brand B bread	1 loaf	$2.15
Bargain Hut	Brand C ground beef	1 pound	$1.99 per lb

On the list, write down the store name, the item, the item's size and the cost. One easy way to do this is by using columns. Write the store name in the left-hand column, and each item under the appropriate heading.

Step 2
A Week in Your Life

As you make a shopping list, look ahead to the week or two for which you are buying groceries. Is there one night where everyone will be attending an event and won't get home until almost 7:00 p.m.? That's probably not the best night to plan a meal that requires a lot of preparation. It's better to allow for something that can be assembled quickly or reheated for that night. Be smart and save the recipes that require more preparation for days when you have the time to put into it.

Other things to consider are what you already have in your pantry, refrigerator or freezer. If you have a couple of frozen chicken breasts from last week, find a recipe that calls for a few cups of diced cooked chicken. Did the neighbor leave you some zucchini from her garden? How can you use that this week? Remember, you don't have to make gourmet-style meals with expensive ingredients every night of the week. Most families enjoy tried-and-true recipes that have evolved into favorites over time.

Step 3 Recipe Research

Once you've got a list of items on sale this week, you'll need to see how they fit together in some budget-friendly recipes. All the recipes included in this book use ingredients that are typically low cost and work well to feed a family of four. Many of the ingredients are common to other recipes as well, so you can pair up recipes to use in the same week—they'll share many of the same ingredients but are different enough to provide a delicious variety for your family.

You can also use some of your family favorites as long as you keep in mind the three basic rules of a budget recipe:

» high yield
» low number of ingredients
» low cost per ingredient

With practice, you'll find yourself automatically examining

recipes to see how you can reduce the cost. I usually draw a little chart for each day of the week and write the ingredients down for each meal. It helps me to visualize what I need and fleshes out my grocery list.

As you are looking for budget-friendly recipes, remember that each night doesn't have to be a gourmet-quality dining experience. Keep things simple. I find that my family is the most satisfied with humble, filling meals. I have eight or ten meals that are consistently their favorites, and I work one or two of them in each week on a rotating basis. Save the labor-intensive meals for special nights or perhaps schedule one for a single night

each week. There are plenty of ways to make simple meals feel special—it just takes a little time and creativity.

Also, think about recipes that would be easy to double and freeze. Pasta and many casseroles don't take any extra time to double, they freeze well and can be a real life-saver down the road. As you're planning a weekly menu, it's

TUESDAY— TUNA PATTIES

3 cans tuna

(already have crackers at home?)

1 egg

(already have hamburger buns at home?)

MONDAY— 5 CAN CHILI

1 can black beans

1 can Northern beans

2 cans chili beans in sauce

(already have 1 can diced tomatoes at home?)

(already have chili powder at home?)

important to factor in what meals you might already have made, or what you can make in the coming week that can be doubled to use next week.

Step 4
Re-examine the List

After you've put together a list of groceries (including the ingredients from the meals you will be making), review it. Is there something you can cut out, combine or consolidate? I'll tell you later some specific ways how to do this, but for now be smart. Do you always have leftover chicken when you make your mother's recipe for chicken and rice? Make that on Tuesday, then use the leftover chicken for quesadillas on Thursday and eliminate that expensive salmon dinner you had scheduled. After a few weeks of smart shopping and thrifty cooking, you'll start to see places on your grocery list where you can really "trim the fat."

Step 5 Where to Shop

You can always get a lot of advice on where to shop. Perhaps your cousin swears by the mega-warehouse store and your mother chooses to stick with the locally owned grocery store. Most people go to the supermarket that is the most convenient for them. Depending on your personal situation, there are a few options out there to get the most bang for your grocery buck.

Remember the list you made when you were reviewing the weeklies for the best deals around town? When you divide the shopping list by store, you've automatically given yourself a guide on where to go to get the best prices for the week. When it's time to go shopping, plan your trips accordingly and just purchase what's on the list at each store. Depending on where they are located, you will likely have to improvise. It's not worth spending a dollar in gas to save twenty-five cents on grapes unless you can combine trips, or you're planning to be in that neighborhood for something else. Usually, you can stick to two stores and get the most out of your shopping.

There is one feature that some grocery stores offer that can save you even more time and effort—price matching. Get ready to pick up the phone—it's time to do some detective work. Find the phone numbers of the grocery stores in your area and ask the customer service desk if that store honors price matching. If they do, you're in luck, because your shopping just got easier. In fact, it might be worth driving a little bit farther to a store that does this.

Price matching is what it sounds like—a store will match the price of a product as advertised by any competitor. If the store says they do honor price matching, ask them what they need to confirm it. My grocery store merely requires the name of the competitor store and the sale price of the item. Since I've already scanned all the weekly flyers for all the stores and included them on my grocery list, it's easy to provide that info.

Here's an example of how price matching works. Say that Jane is preparing her weekly menu and shopping list. As she is reading the flyers and making notes, she sees that Market A is selling the house brand of milk at three gallons for $5. She also sees that Market B's advertisement shows some name-brand microwave popcorn for a really great price—just $1.49 per box.

Now, Jane really likes shopping at Market C for many reasons—it's closest to her house, they have a great selection of store-brand products, and they honor price matching. So when it's time to grocery shop, Jane heads to Market C. While she's there, she gets three gallons of house-brand milk and the brand-name popcorn. At the checkout stand, Jane informs the checker before she scans the milk that it is a price match item. Jane confirms that Market A's milk is three for $5. The checker makes the adjustment and the milk rings up at three for $5. As the checker gets to the popcorn, Jane lets her know that the same brand is selling at Market B for $1.49 and the checker makes the proper adjustments to price match the item. In short, price matching allows you to shop at just one store yet take advantage of the sale prices all around town. As long as the brand and package size are the same, the store should honor the competitor's price with no problems. It's a busy person's greatest tool when it comes to saving on groceries.

The warehouse stores are another great place to shop and save, but they are not always the bargain wonders they appear to be. When you compare grocery items by unit price, you can really tell the savings versus the rip-offs. Usually the shelf price tag will display an amount that says "unit price" or "price per unit." Use that number to compare similar products. Even if the savings seem minimal, like $0.20 off each box of generic macaroni and cheese, when you add it all up, it could equal hundreds of dollars each year. The savings almost always cover the cost of the membership fees, but there are a few things to keep in mind when shopping for warehouse bulk items.

» There are actually some items that cost more per unit in bulk, so check the price per unit very carefully.

» Product variety is often limited, so don't settle for seemingly cheap brand-names when the grocery store generic brand is a better buy. Warehouse stores often do not carry generic brands, so while the warehouse prices may be better for brand-name products from the supermarket, they still may be more expensive than a grocery store's house brand.

» Don't buy items that you will not use up before they go to waste. For example, you might be getting a great price on an extra-large can of peaches, but if you open the can, you'd better make sure you'll use or freeze all the peaches you don't consume over a few days.

» The temptation to over-spend is huge, so make sure you aren't using money for six months of mayonnaise now that might need to go for bills next week.

» If you live in a rural area that is far away from a warehouse club, calculate gas and other costs into the overall savings. It may or may not be worth it, unless you can combine trips when you are traveling to that area anyhow.

Alternative stores can often have great bargains, but make sure you aren't burning up gasoline and time scooting around town to save a few pennies. Asian, Latino and Indian markets are often great places to get deals on beans, rice and spices especially.

Sometimes, they will also carry produce that is a lot cheaper than the local supermarkets. If you have local farmers markets, you may want to check them out as well as different fruits and veggies come into season.

What About Coupons and Rebates?

Several years ago, I decided to start using all the high-yield shopping rules I'd heard and read about—rebates, clipping coupons, price matching and so on. There are Web sites, books and magazines dedicated to the high-savings shopper, and the stories of incredible savings are really inspiring. It was easy to envision spending only $40 a week on groceries while my mailbox filled up with little checks from rebates and tons of free samples. However, I soon found that after clipping and filling out forms, I was spending way too much time actually shopping and thinking about shopping. It was then that I decided to design grocery shopping to best fit my life. It's true that I was saving money the other way, but I was losing my sanity.

I compromised and bent the shopping rules to find some kind of balance I could live with. I evolved into a casual coupon clipper, and once I did this, I noticed an immediate reduction in stress yet still managed to keep my grocery budget in a manageable place. In short, some people are meant to be coupon clippers and some are not. While some find it frustrating and time-consuming to clip coupons

for everything, there are those who do it and love it. Try some of these simple experiments to see how you react:

Check the house brand first— For kitchen basics, the house brand is often less expensive than the brand-name item with a coupon. It makes no budget shopping sense to buy condensed cream of chicken soup in a brand-name can with a coupon when the house brand is still ten cents less than that. Make sure you are happy with the quality of the house brand. Some items have no notice-able difference in quality or texture, but a few items seem to be remarkably inferior. Just experiment to find what your family likes and dislikes.

Look inside and on the packaging— Many products have coupons right on them or tucked away inside. Your favorite bread may have a cou-pon inside each loaf at the very bottom of the bag, making the bread price less than even the house brand.

Establish need— Just because you have a coupon doesn't mean you have to buy it. If it's an item you normally don't purchase, getting it at a reduced price still means you're spending outside of your budget to get it.

Cheaper from scratch— Often there are coupons for prepackaged meals and stovetop helpers, but you can avoid them because their equivalent can generally be made from scratch at about half the cost.

Double coupons— Check to see if any of the stores in your area offer double coupon deals. That's when the store matches the coupon, so you get double the amount off the purchase price. This may make some items that seem too expensive suddenly very affordable.

Is It Worth It?

For those who are new at food budgeting, this may seem like quite a lot to do. However, with a few weeks of practice, you'll find that you're planning meals like a pro, and you'll notice several other things:

» You're spending less time at the store for your initial shopping run.

» You are eliminating those midweek "I-forgot-something" trips back to the stores where you'll overspend.

» You are less stressed when it comes to meal prep time because you know exactly what's on the menu.

» You're grocery bill is getting smaller every week as you learn more about budget shopping and meal planning.

» Your family will have more variety in what they like to eat.

» You'll spend less on last-minute take-out dinners.

Imagine if you could save just $30 each week off the grocery bill—a conservative estimate. That's a total savings of $1,680 each year. Wouldn't it be great to put that toward a family vacation, retirement or to pay off debts? That's great savings for doing something that only takes a couple of hours each week. It's like a little income boost, but you don't have to pay taxes on your "earnings." Because shopping and cooking are things that need to be done anyhow, a little extra effort can result in big rewards.

Price List

For people who are really serious about cutting their food budget, the price list is a must. With very little effort, you can save lots of money each month, and the process is so simple that it hardly interferes with regular meal planning.

A price list is a record of the best prices for the items you regularly buy. As a list of prices, it keeps you educated on what the best prices are, not just what the store informs you is a great sale price. Most shoppers are familiar with some of the basic sales pitches: buy one, get one free; ten for $10; and more. However, stores are in the business to make money and are counting on the fact that you'll believe them when they tell you that $3 per pound for ground beef is a good deal because it's marked down from $3.99. Without a price list, you might believe that you are truly saving a dollar per pound! The buy-one-get-one-free sales also make shoppers feel as if the stores are practically giving away food. If you don't know the real price of one item, you might be surprised to learn that the "sale" price is usually marked up extremely high to compensate for the "free" item.

A price list is your best friend when it comes to knowing if a store is trying to sell an overpriced product by giving you a false basis for comparison. When your price book reminds you that you've purchased ground beef for $2 per pound before, the $3 per pound isn't such a hot deal anymore. The price book is your own personal record of sale prices and

DATE	STORE	ITEM	SIZE	UNIT PRICE	PRICE
3/10	SJ	Milk	1 gallon	--	$2.88/gallon
3/10	SJ	Bread	20 ounce (1 loaf)	$0.09/ounce	$1.88/loaf
4/2	WM	Ground Beef	1 pound	$0.16/ounce	$2.33/pound
4/25	WM	Soda	2 liters	--	$1.09/bottle
4/25	WM	Tomatoes	per pound	$0.07/ounce	$1.25/pound
5/26	T	Sugar	1 pound	$0.14	$2.35/pound

regular prices. You'll be armed with the knowledge of which sales are really good deals and which ones are inflated.

It might seem like a real chore to write down every price for every item you buy. It's not that hard, and the knowledge and power that comes with the education is really the key to saving money at the grocery stores each week. It'll help you cruise through the weekly flyers and assess what really is a good deal and what isn't. You'll also have an easier time in tracking price cycles and seasonal sales.

Stores anticipate that most of their customers don't take the time to remember prices and that they'll be persuaded to get these "great sales" because the advertising tells them to. Don't be fooled and you can save a lot of money.

Starting a Price List

There are as many techniques for a price list as there are smart shoppers, so you'll eventually come up with your own way that works the best for you. There are local and regional online clubs that you can join that will send you information on the hottest sales for the week. You can even download price list charts and checklists from various grocery guru Web sites. However, if you are just beginning, start simply and expand from there as you see the results.

All you need for now is a spiral notebook and pen. On the first page, write column headings for the date, store, item, size, price, unit price and sale price. Start with basic items such as milk, bread, ground beef and so forth.

Date— This is important because it'll help you track the cycles of the item's sales, generally a few months apart.
Store— Where you purchased the item, whether at a traditional grocery store, dented-can outlet or day-old bakery. Many people develop codes for stores using initials.
Item— Be specific with brand name and special flavors/variations.
Size— The ounces per bag or can, pounds or total yield.
Unit size— Very important in determining bargains between brands as it tells how much you are paying per pound or ounce. While many items are uniformly packaged (most large containers of milk are

1 gallon and 2-liter bottles of soda are exactly 2 liters) some food items are packaged differently. Thus you can compare a 15-ounce bag of chips with an 18-ounce bag and see which one is less expensive per ounce. Sale price— Try to get the actual price to the penny, and don't estimate.

Fill in the information at home with as many weekly flyers as you can, as it'll save you time at the store, but you should always bring the notebook along with you to the store. Realize that this is a work in progress and your first foray will feel strange. You'll need a few weeks to really build up a list and note the variations in prices from week to week.

Using the Price Guide

Each time you need to buy an item, consult the price guide and see what you've paid before. If the newest price is lower, erase the old price and write in the new overall price and unit price. As you purchase additional food (and even nonfood) items, you can add them to the list. The goal is to eventually make sure that you are purchasing the item

for the lowest prices. If you can't find the item at the lowest price in your price guide, skip it or decide if you must have it.

For example, if you come across a 20-ounce can of chunked pineapple on sale for $1.29, you'd consult the price guide to see what the lowest price for that has been. When you see that you bought some a few weeks ago for $0.99 a can, you know that the sale price isn't as good as it could be. You can then decide to buy the item or pass.

A price guide will also make meal planning easier as you figure out how to incorporate the really inexpensive items into your menus. If you usually put broccoli in a certain casserole dish, but the green beans are on sale for a rock-bottom price per can, then substitute the more expensive ingredient with the cheaper one. Within a month or two, you'll soon learn which items fluctuate in price and which ones are fairly steady.

Now, all prices will increase over time, and you'll need to adjust for that over the years. Also, prices on produce can vary due to natural reasons, such as a late frost or flooding.

However, the price list can still be used as a week-to-week and month-to-month guide.

With a complete price guide, the goal is to never pay more than the lowest price. When you find a great sale, stock up with as much as you can afford, and you'll have the item on hand for whenever you need it. You'll also be more educated on how to buy in bulk. When you see that sugar prices are down to $1 per 5-pound bag, you can stock up at that great price and use your low-priced sugar long after the price climbs back up.

The price guide allows you to critically analyze the sales and get the most for your money. You can compare the price per unit from one package to the other. For example, a smart spender will know from the price guide that the 15-ounce bag of potato chips on sale at Store A is a great deal compared to the 13-ounce bag of potato chips at Store B. If you notice that a certain brand name of potato chip seems to be sitting solidly at a good price while all the competitors have gone up, double-check the weight. Chances are the company has lowered the weight of the product, so you are paying the same price for less.

You aren't always going to find the lowest prices every time you go shopping—that's a fact. However, with a price guide, you can be educated on which sales are good and which prices are true bargains. When used in tandem with sales, coupons and price matching, the price book will be the most valuable tool you have in cutting your monthly grocery bills by hundreds of dollars.

Chapter 2
At the Store

Many times at the grocery store, shoppers fall into a pattern of behavior. They start at the same end of the store, walk the same route inside and even go through the same checkout line. They seldom deviate. It's time to wake up and take control of your grocery shopping experience. As you become more supermarket savvy, saving money will get easier.

Even if you are armed with the best-ever shopping list, it's tough to get in and out of the store as planned without a whole lot of will power. Things such as store layout, time of day, your state of mind and really powerful marketing psychology techniques are at work, encouraging you to spend more money.

General Shopping Tips

Once you've determined which supermarket or warehouse club you'll be shopping at, you're ready to go. Try to choose a time when you can go with the least distractions. If you can, have your spouse stay home with the kids or swap babysitting time with a friend. It'll be worth it to allow you to concentrate. However, it can be nice to have an older child accompany you—it provides some good one-on-one time, and it's a good opportunity to teach them about money and smart shopping. If you must take children, try to turn it into a game or treasure hunt. Children can be surprisingly entertained when it comes to comparing prices.

It's also helpful to go when the stores are not crowded but are well stocked. When there are too many people jammed in each aisle, you will feel more in a hurry to toss in whatever will suffice and get out of there sooner. Some like to go early in the morning, but others may think that a late-night trip is just the ticket. Generally, avoid the after-work, pre-dinner crush and anytime after 11:00 a.m. on Saturdays and Sundays.

Go to the grocery store as infrequently as you can. Most people go once a week, as this coincides with the weekly flyers, lets you restock on fresh produce and milk, and generally is easier to budget from paycheck to paycheck. The easiest way to blow your food budget is to dash into the store once or twice more per week for a few items and leave with three times as many. Simply make do with what you have at home, modify a recipe if you've forgotten something or do without—it'll save money every month.

Another way to control spending at the store is to be savvy to the well-researched techniques that grocery stores try to entice you with. Here are some of the clever strategies that try to convince you to spend more:

» **Enticing smells:** Have you ever noticed that the bakeries are often located near the front entrance and they always have something yummy in the oven? It's designed to make you hungry when you enter the store and hopefully cause you to do some impulse buying.

Solution: Either don't shop when you're hungry or drink a large glass of water beforehand to take the edge off your appetite.

» Store layout: There's a reason why the milk is always in the back corner of the store. If you're just dashing in for milk but wander past aisles of well-stocked groceries, there's always a chance you'll see something else you need. Several dollars later, you've spent too much again.
Solution: Make a well-planned single trip to avoid midweek store runs.

» Product placement: Know that many marketing dollars have been spent figuring out that this is a big factor in grocery shopping. Generally a store will place the brand-name products on the middle, or eye-level, shelves. Rushed shoppers tend to grab whatever is in front of them, but relaxed shoppers look for the bargains. Because shelf space is at a premium, stores want to get as much as they can from the higher-priced spaces.
Solution: Look low and high for the house brands and less expensive brands.

» Aisle displays: Don't be fooled by the end-of-aisle displays. Although they might be arranged to look like a sale, often the products placed here are simply being promoted more than others—again appealing to casual shoppers.
Solution: Stick to the price list to determine the real sales. Sometimes the sales really are set up at the aisle's end, but don't count on this to be true every time.

» Product appearance: Since bright colors and fancy packaging are attractive, shoppers tend to pick up these items first. House brands are generally much less colorful. However, just because a well-designed soup can or cereal box catches your eye doesn't mean you have to buy it.
Solution: Stay focused on the price of the item, not the packaging it comes in.

» Checkout: It's a retailer's dream to have you sit and stare at the products on a shelf for five to fifteen minutes with nothing else to do. The checkout aisle is crammed with as many items as possible to ensure that you will add at least one or two to your grocery cart.

Solution: Stick to the list. A big budget-buster is impulse buying—when you spontaneously buy something regardless of price. When you pick up something that isn't on your list, ask yourself why you want it. Do you need it and you just forgot to add it to the list? Is it a great unadvertised sale? Are you hungry and you plan to eat it in the car on the way home? Are your children bugging you to buy it? Analyze what drove you to pick the item up. Too many impulse purchases can wreck your carefully planned food budget.

Aisle-by-Aisle Shopping Strategies

By learning how stores influence a customer's shopping and spending habits, you are in possession of some very valuable knowledge. Keep in mind the strategies and tips on how to offset the grocery store's selling techniques and you control your grocery spending more than ever before. Be active in making purchases and, with practice, you'll soon be lowering your weekly food budget.

Produce

It might seem that fresh fruits and vegetables don't belong on a budget-conscious grocery list because they seem too expensive and often go to waste before a family can eat them. While it's true that fresh fruits and vegetables take some careful attention, they are an important part of a menu, and combined with frozen and canned produce, can still be included in even the most frugal plan.

The cheapest vegetables—generally potatoes, cabbage, broccoli, whole carrots, onions and sweet potatoes—are wonderful items to incorporate into a family menu. The cheapest fruits—generally apples, bananas, papayas, melons and grapefruits—are also family-friendly. When certain fruits and vegetables are in season, they become extremely inexpensive, often half what they'd normally cost. For example, when corn on the cob is in season, you can often buy plenty of fresh ears for $1. Don't even think about trying to find inexpensive corn on the cob in the off-season.

It is a huge advantage to know which fruits and vegetables are in season, whether locally or imported from other countries. Not only are they less expensive, but they'll be fresher, too. Spring is the time for asparagus, beets, citrus fruits, cucumbers, honeydew melons, peas, new potatoes, radishes, strawberries and rhubarb. Look for all kinds of berries, cantaloupe, summer produce, tomatoes, tropical fruits, eggplants, peppers, watermelon and zucchini in summer. Autumn brings apples, cabbage, cauliflower, pears, pumpkins, squashes and grapes. The winter season provides fresh imports such as oranges, clementines, kiwi fruit, pineapples, sweet potatoes and other tropical fruits.

Get familiar with which vegetables and fruits are less expensive when fresh and which ones are less expensive when frozen or canned. Incorporate them into your recipes and substitute when you need to. Bear in mind that taste and texture can be a deal-breaker when it comes to alternatives, though. For example, my family can't stand canned peas but we love frozen peas. Even though canned peas are generally cheaper, I don't buy them. I spend a little more for peas that my family will eat rather than let canned peas go to waste.

Even though fruits and vegetables might seem expensive to incorporate into your family's eating habits, when compared to other snacks and sides, they're healthier and actually work out to be less costly than the sugary or salty alternatives. Try carrot sticks as a side instead of potato chips, or a cup of fruit salad rather than processed sugary cakes and cookies. When you start substituting fruits and veggies for junk food, both your grocery bill and your family's health will improve.

Beware of the conveniently packaged produce, designed to save time in preparation. Anything from prepackaged salads to baby carrots often cost double what it takes to make them from scratch. As a rule, the closer the food is to its natural state, the less expensive it is. Buy whole carrots and spend five minutes chopping them yourself or with the kids. Spend $1 on a melon baller and dig in. What you spend in time results in big savings.

Finally, use all the produce you purchase. It's a real waste to spend money on fresh produce then throw it away at the end of the week. Even if you've found a bunch of bananas on sale, you've still lost money if you have to toss them because they are turning brown. Use brown and spotted bananas in a fruit smoothie or in banana-nut bread, and then nothing has gone to waste. Most vegetables and many fruits freeze well, so when in doubt, put it on ice and you've stretched your grocery dollars successfully.

Meat, Poultry and Fish

Perhaps one of the most costly parts of a family's food budget is meat, poultry and fish. The simplest way to cut a food budget is to go 100 percent vegetarian, but most families (including mine) aren't willing to do this. However, there are a lot of ways that you can incorporate dishes that include meat that won't make you cringe every time you step up to the butcher's block.

The first thing to realize is that not every meal has to include meat. Plan for one or two meatless dishes every week. There are thousands of vegetarian recipes out there, so find the ones that are filling and inexpensive. If you aren't buying cuts of meat for each meal, you'll see big savings almost immediately.

Look for cheaper cuts of meat and get familiar with which ones work in recipes you already have. Many people avoid cheaper cuts because they believe they aren't as flavorful or might be a bit tougher. Of course, a sirloin steak is always going to taste more fantastic than stew beef, but when it comes to saving money, the stew beef is the right choice. One secret to tasty cuts of meat is marinades—acid-based flavorings that tenderize the meat. Another way to get the most out of less expensive cuts of meat is by cooking them low and slow, as in a slow cooker.

In general, try to choose one red meat item each week that is on sale, whether it's a pot roast, ground beef, pork or lamb, and stretch it as far as you can. With a roast, you will likely be able to use leftover meat for two or three meals afterward, such as in chili or soup. When you are looking for recipes, seek out the ones where meat isn't the star. Rather, choose delicious recipes where meat is a complement to the overall dish.

Keep an eye out for sales on ham, especially during holidays, as they tend to go on incredible sales. Ham is one of those things that seems to last and last, and ends up adding to at least four or five meals along the way. Even though a ham seems expensive on initial purchase, with a good sale a ham can be one of the best bargains for meat, pound for pound. Pork chops are generally inexpensive as well, and many steak dishes and recipes can substitute pork chops with no problems.

Poultry, specifically chicken, is one of the most versatile yet least expensive meats around. It's also the food item whose price seems to yo-yo the most. After a few weeks of keeping a price list, you'll soon learn the best sale price in your area for chicken. When chicken goes on sale, buy more than is needed. Since boneless, skinless chicken breasts are generally the most expensive, look for whole chicken or other cuts of chicken to save money. If you really insist on the boneless, skinless breasts, seek out recipes that call for cooked cubed chicken, rather than whole breasts per serving, to stretch the poultry a little further each week.

The slow cooker is key to having prepared chicken at a moment's notice. When you purchase chicken, pop it into the slow cooker all day with a little water. By the end of the day, spend a few minutes pulling the meat off the bones or otherwise chopping and slicing the meat as needed. Put approximately two cups of cubed or shredded chicken into freezer-safe bags and freeze until needed. Most budget recipes that include poultry call for 2 cups cooked cubed or shredded chicken. For the extra frugal, save the bones to make your own chicken broth.

Look for sales on poultry, especially for turkey around the winter holidays. If you have the freezer space, buy an extra gobbler or two, as turkey can be substituted for chicken in just about any recipe. Ground turkey is a great substitute for ground beef in many recipes, and it doesn't cost nearly as much and contains a lot less fat.

Pork is another meat that seems to swing wildly in price. Although it is flavorful and versatile, for some reason, many people pass it by when they are seeking out recipes to fit the budget. Look for recipes that utilize pork, such as pork loin, pork chops and more, and stock up when this meat goes on sale.

Fish is generally one of the most expensive meats, even if you live close to the ocean. Fish fillets, crab and shrimp are almost universally too expensive when it comes to a thrifty grocery plan. However, there are always exceptions, and if your family loves fish, watch for sales and never buy it at regular price. Try various kinds of fish on sale, rather than choosing something like salmon steaks at regular price.

Seafood actually has seasonal highs and lows, with spring and summer showing price reductions in salmon soft-shelled crabs, lobster, halibut and sea bass. Fall and winter offer lower prices for shellfish, swordfish and squid.

Buying meat in bulk is another way to gain great savings. It only takes a few minutes to take a 10-pound package of ground beef and divide it into ten 1-pound freezer storage bags. You'll benefit from the savings and have just the right amount for cooking. Try this divide-and-conquer technique with bulk meats such as pork chops, chicken drumsticks and more.

One of the best secret weapons for buying meat is to check out the reduced sale bin in the meat department. This is where the store places meat that is set to expire within the week. If you can't find the bin, ask the store butcher. Sometimes the reduced-sale cuts are left with the regularly priced meats but are marked with special stickers or other identifying marks. These prime cuts of meats are often marked anywhere from 40 to 80 percent off. Smart shoppers always check out the sale bin and pick up some of the choicest cuts for pennies on the pound. Make sure you use the meat before the expiration date or else freeze it until you are ready. Frozen meat can safely store for 6 to 12 months or even longer if it is packaged in freezer bags, freezer paper or heavy-duty aluminum foil, so stock up when you see a great bargain in the reduced sale bin. This way, you can eat steak for the same price as regular hamburger.

Finally, when it comes to meat, you must readjust your thinking on how much meat your family actually needs. Does each family member eat three or four helpings of meat at each meal? If so, adjust the meal so they fill up on veggies, salads or breads instead and stick to one or two helpings of the meat. Will the recipe suffer if you use ½ pound of ground beef instead of 1 pound? Choose delicious recipes where meat is the supporting ingredient to the overall dish.

Bread, Cereal, Pasta and Grains

This group has some of the least expensive options around, and the good news is that many are healthy and filling. Most of the time, the generic versions of these are pretty tasty and really inexpensive. No matter if you are buying the house brand or a brand name, make sure the bread or pasta you are purchasing is really a healthy upgrade. Health-conscious shoppers are usually interested in buying whole wheat bread and pasta, but read the packaging carefully. It must actually say 100 percent whole wheat.

If the packaging says that is "contains 100 percent whole wheat," "wheat bread," "uses wheat flour," or even plain "wheat blend" bread or pasta, it usually means that there is less than the full amount of whole wheat. If you are going to pay more for it, make sure it has the nutritional punch you're looking for.

Bread—Generally, for muffins, biscuits and rolls, using extremely inexpensive mixes available are just about the most cost effective when it comes to saving time and money. Look for generic mixes and store-brand refrigerated and frozen varieties. When it comes to bagels, tortillas, hot dog buns and hamburger buns, try the lowest-priced brands first. If you get no complaints, great! If your family doesn't like them for some reason, try the next lowest priced.

Another way to save on breads is to find a discount bakery or outlet store in your area. You'll often find that bread, rolls and more are usually at least half price and the bread is generally no more than a day or two older than in the supermarket. Plan a trip to go once a month, buy five or six loaves, along with rolls, tortillas and pastries, and freeze what you won't use right away. By wrapping them in heavy-duty aluminum foil and then placing them in freezer storage bags, they'll keep for up to three months. This is a great place to get cookies and snacks that you normally would pay top dollar for at the grocery store.

Cereal—This is one area where coupons really bring in big savings and supermarkets will often put cereal in their loss-leader advertisements as a "buy one, get one free" or "five for $10." In combination, it's possible to get brand-name boxes of cereal for $2 or less every time. Stock up when the sales are on or visit the warehouse clubs because they'll often have great prices on bulk cereal. Always compare the cost per unit. Some retailers assume customers will always buy the bigger cereal box over the smaller one, but you'll often find that the larger box is the more expensive per unit. As always, check out the house-brand bagged cereals, which often taste just as good for much less (even with a great coupon).

Consider serving your family something else for breakfast, such as pancakes, waffles, eggs or oatmeal. These breakfast items are sometimes less expensive per plate than cold cereal, so if you can eliminate a few bowls of cereal each week, you can save a little more at the store.

Pasta—While brand names tend to go on sale, it seems that the house brands and the warehouse club options are the best for pasta. This pantry item can be stored for up to a year on a cupboard shelf and is a staple in a budget-conscious diet. With so many varieties of noodles available, don't just settle for plain and straight. Instead of spaghetti, try some different shapes and textures to transform a humdrum pasta dish into something new and interesting.

You might be tempted to buy the quick prepackaged meals that feature pasta and require you to "add your own meat." Not only are these quickie meals not as healthy as those made from scratch, but they are also more expensive. You can easily make two similar meals from scratch for roughly the same cost.

Grains—Rice, couscous and bulgur are just a few of the possibilities in the grain aisle at the grocery store. Stock up when they are on sale, and look for bulk purchases here, too. Stay away from the tiny, flavored rice boxes. With plenty of sodium and other additives, you're spending way too much for a less-than-healthy side dish. Look for brown rice as a cup for cup substitute in recipes that call for cooked white rice, and experiment with other grains as well.

The harvest cycles have some impact on the price of grains; however, most grain commodities depend on annual cycles. In recent years, the price of grains has skyrocketed due to a combination of agricultural, financial and energy problems, everything dependent upon grains, such as feed for cattle. Make the most of grain purchases by hunting for bargains and making your selections as healthy as possible so you get the most nutritional bang for your buck.

Dairy

I think having my own milk cow would sometimes be less expensive than buying milk every week. Because my family would drink their weight in milk and consume entire blocks of cheese every day if they could, I find that dairy is one of the toughest items to purchase consistently within my budget allowance.

The good news is that milk is usually on sale somewhere near you, and with price matching, a smart shopper can usually get a pretty good deal. Also, drugstores and convenience stores will often run sales on gallons of milk that are surprisingly great. While milk really does a body good, there are ways to make it stretch a little further. For example, serve milk at every mealtime and with cereal, but encourage family members to drink water between meals. Studies show that most people, including kids, don't get nearly enough water each day, so if kids are thirsty, water will do the job more quickly than milk. Also, use evaporated milk or powdered milk for cooking and save the fresh stuff for drinking. Milk varies in price between fat content, so keep track of which type your family likes and note when it is on sale.

Cheese is another dairy item that seems to break the bank. The best deals are often with coupons or at the warehouse clubs. Shredded cheese freezes well and can be added to recipes while frozen, but purchasing bagged shredded cheese is almost always more expensive per ounce than a block of the same cheese. Look for blocks of cheese and plan to shred and bag smaller portions to save money since the presliced, shredded or individually wrapped cheeses are the most expensive.

Think of it this way. What does it cost you to buy a 1-pound block of cheddar for $6 and shred it yourself rather than buy a pound of shredded cheese for $9? If the shredding takes about two minutes to complete, then you've just saved that $3 difference with a few minutes of work. Spend a little time to save a lot of money.

Try substituting cheese flavors in recipes to take advantage of varieties that are on sale. For example, buy a large block of Colby Jack with a coupon and use that cheese in your recipes all week rather than purchasing three different kinds of cheese. Another idea is to purchase a different block of cheese on sale every week, and then shred, bag and freeze it. Whenever you need a certain type of cheese, go to your own freezer rather than pay top dollar at the store.

Eggs, located near the dairy section, also vary wildly in price from week to week. Most people will never be able to taste the difference between egg "brands" so look for the cheapest. Compare unit prices to see if you're better off getting a 12-count or 18-count box. It's a good idea to avoid egg substitutes, as they are quite pricey, unless you must for health reasons.

Frozen Foods

The frozen food section is the home of some of the best grocery bargains as well as some of the worst. The smart shopper can really be tested here, so make sure you are armed with enough knowledge to get through the traps and find the treasure.

First, know that convenience food comes with a price. Although this is true for many different food items throughout the store, it is rarely more evident than in the frozen food section. With prepackaged and flash-frozen items that just require you to thaw and cook, the convenience factor looms large. However, many of these convenience foods are not that much more convenient than if you made a double batch from scratch one night and froze the other portion. Instead of purchasing individual frozen dinners, make and freeze individual portions yourself. Don't buy that tiny frozen lasagna—make your own, double the recipe and enjoy the savings. Steer clear of frozen pancakes and waffles. Instead make a double or triple batch from scratch and freeze the leftovers. You'll be able to pop them in the microwave or toaster anytime for a quick hot breakfast or snack.

There are some budget-friendly prepared foods in the frozen food section that may, on occasion, come to the rescue when your dinner plans don't always work out. There are sometimes great sales on pot pies and frozen pizzas that are hard to beat. Also, consider that there are times when a fun frozen pizza or two can be just as filling as two delivery pizzas for more than twice the cost. If you regularly order out for pizza, look at some of the gourmet options in the frozen food section. With a combination of sales and coupons, these fun foods can be a surprisingly cost-effective replacement for a fast-food jaunt—just don't depend on them for daily meals. Remember that, as a rule, prepared frozen meals are not very cost effective and usually will not be as nutritious as your homemade meals.

On the flip side, there are some frozen foods that are a budget shopper's dream come true. For example, frozen vegetables and fruit often cost much less than fresh or canned, and you might be surprised to know that they are often healthier because the vitamin content is preserved when they are flash frozen. Compare this to their fresh counterparts that have been picked a week or so ago, trucked or transported and left to sit on the grocery store shelf. After all that, the vitamin content drops significantly. Besides, a bag of frozen veggies or fruit lasts much longer in a freezer than in a pantry, minimizing the chances of waste.

Frozen treats are generally very high in price and low in

yield. Frozen cakes, pies and some kinds of ice cream are extremely expensive, especially when you consider that you can make other desserts, even frozen ones, for a fraction of the cost.

Finally, evaluate each frozen item on its own merits. Ask yourself if you can get the same food elsewhere in a different form. Can you make it from scratch for less, or can you make double the amount for the same price as the frozen version? Do you have the freezer space for the item? Soon you'll be familiar enough with which frozen food items will help you on your way to a lower grocery bill.

Bakery and Snacks

Everyone loves snacks, and it's easy to spend a lot on salty and sugary items. For the most part, you can keep snack foods on your grocery list with some wise shopping skills and portion control at home.

For potato chips, buy the store brand that offers the best unit price. When you get home, repackage them in single serving portions in zippered bags. They'll be great for sack lunches and snacks.

The temptation to keep eating and eating from a large bag is nearly impossible for anyone to resist. Look for generic pretzels and crackers as inexpensive alternatives to potato chips.

There are some things that the bakery can provide that you probably cannot make at home, such as fancy birthday cakes and donuts. However, stay far away from the bakery if you are serious about saving money. Check out a discount or outlet bakery for little lunch box snack items for the kids, or check out the day-old rack, as you can often get some pretty fancy desserts for well under half price. Then freeze or serve within a few days. Generally, you will be able to find rolls and bakery snacks at bakery discount stores at a much better price, and you can make muffins from inexpensive mixes for less than buying from a bakery.

Chapter 3
In the Kitchen

When it comes to preparing and serving meals to your family, remember that you are in control of the kitchen. As long as you present an attractive and delicious meal, you are less likely to get any complaints. Instead, you'll be pleased to see everyone clean their plates and compliment you on a tasty dinner. Nobody has to know exactly what goes on behind the scenes.

When implementing budget cooking tips, start with the ones that you can introduce without causing major upheaval in the family. Don't declare that meals will now be vegetarian in order to save money—most likely, that news won't be welcomed. Instead, serve a carefully researched meatless dish and see how they like it. Rather than informing everyone that you've reduced a particular ingredient or made tonight's soup from leftovers, simply smile and serve the meal and evaluate the reactions. Start with a few things and keep adding; as you move toward better meals as a result of better planning, your smile will be genuine.

As you learn which recipes your family enjoys, make a master list or a special recipe box for budget meals so you can refer back to them for reminders and ideas. Scour cookbooks for qualified recipes and mark them or recopy them. Some people create binders for favorites, while others mark the pages. However you decide to accumulate budget recipes, make sure you keep trying to find ones that are delicious, healthy and low

cost. The recipes included in this book are a great place to start, and there are some pages in the back to add more of your own.

20 Budget Cooking Tips
Recipes

» Know your family's likes and dislikes. If they absolutely won't eat yams, not even the best sale price in the world makes yams worth buying.

» Look for recipes that require a few inexpensive ingredients and avoid recipes that call for gourmet items or large cuts of meat per person. Also stay away from recipes that require you to buy something you'll rarely use again, such as an exotic spice.

» Save or bookmark recipes that your family really likes or those that yield a lot of leftovers. You can create a running list of recipes or simply note down the cookbook page number and title. This will save time when you're ready to plan a weekly menu.

» Experiment with recipes. If you're making a casserole that calls for carrots, corn and peas, but you're missing the corn, use what you have. There are a handful of vegetables that can be easily substituted for each other in a pinch. The same is true for cooked rice versus other grains.

» Substitute less expensive ingredients for expensive ones. Determine if the recipe absolutely must have that item to make it work. If not, leave it out or else decide if there is a cheaper alternative. For example, exchanging margarine for butter works in many recipes with no noticeable difference.

» If you can't substitute for the expensive ingredient, use less of it. For example, try cutting the amount by a third. Keep cutting each time you make the dish to see how it tastes. Once the adjustment is noticeable, add a little back in until you are satisfied.

» Reduce meat consumption overall. You'll be surprised how little meat you actually need for many recipes. Use ½ to ⅔ pound ground beef when a recipe calls for 1 pound and see how it affects the recipe. Cut the meat or add more vegetables, rice, beans or whatever until your family notices a difference. Chances are, they won't.

Wise Use

» Use everything and think of ways to get every last bit out of whatever you are cooking. From meat bones to leftover rice, there's a way to use it if you are willing.

» Plan for leftovers as a meal for one or two nights. Train yourself to think long-term about the roast you're making and understand that you can use the leftovers for other dishes. It requires a little advanced planning, but you'll thank yourself later. You'll never have to stare at a leftover chunk of meat again, wishing there was something you could do with it.

» The freezer is a great way to keep food longer until you can use it. It helps eliminate waste and can be a real lifesaver on busy nights if you plan ahead, so use your freezer as much as you can. Many budget-conscious people purchase a deep freezer for a few hundred dollars and swear that it pays for itself quickly.

» Invest in basic food storage items. Simple plastic containers with lids, freezer bags and aluminum foil can keep food fresh and protected until you need it again.

Eliminate the Obvious

» Cut down or eliminate junk food. Find more healthy and inexpensive alternatives instead. For example, have flavored water instead of soda, eat dessert every other night instead of every night and stock up on things like pretzels and popcorn instead of chips and doughnuts.

» The average adult eats out for lunch around twice a week. Plan on bringing lunch from home to save big and use up leftovers.

» Cut back visits to restaurants, both sit-down and fast food. Save the fancy restaurants for special events, and avoid fast-food drive-ups and delivery options. With well-planned weekly meals, you won't have to reach for the keys or the phone to get a family meal at the last minute. Instead, you can go to the refrigerator or freezer to create a hot wholesome meal in no time.

» Have a tried-and-true "standby" meal that is always in your pantry, such as the ingredients for tuna melts or chili. When there's simply no time to make anything else or you're running on empty with other ingredients, the standby meal will come to the rescue.

» Bring drinks from home. Making coffee at home is always a better deal than buying it on the go. Same for juice, bottled water and flavored sports drinks. Instead of purchasing them individually from a vending machine or convenience store, bring along a thermos, sports bottle or canister. Even buying these drinks in bulk at the grocery store is less expensive than buying them individually elsewhere.

Health Above All

» Don't sacrifice health for low-cost items. Even though you can feed your family on four packets of ramen noodles every night for a month, there isn't much nutritional value in it. The key is finding nutritious and low-cost meals. You'll spend a lot more on doctor bills and medications when you have a poor diet.

» Think healthy and work low-cost yet nutritious foods into your diet. Bread and pasta that are made with 100 percent whole grains are more filling and healthy than bleached white alternatives. Try brown rice instead of white and have fruits and veggies around instead of chips and cookies.

» Control portions. We tend to eat portions that far exceed what we actually need. Once you begin eating better and getting used to smaller portions, you'll find that you are full on less. Consult nutrition guides for accurate portions and servings.

Don't Throw That Away

Wasting food is a huge drain on the family food budget. You've probably gathered by now that making the food you purchase go as far as you can is one of the key components to reducing spending for the family food budget.

Consider that in an average week, a family can toss out as much as ¼ to ⅓ of the food they buy. If in doubt, just monitor what goes into the garbage can at your house for a day or two. Kids are especially guilty of only eating part of their meals or leaving half a glass of milk. Everything from rotting fruit to spoiled leftovers in the refrigerator adds up.

Imagine this wasteful excess in terms of money. If a family spends $100 on food in a week, that's $33 of food wasted. That extra $33 each week works out to almost $1,720 per year—well worth a little time and energy to cut down on food waste.

Talk with your family on how you can avoid wasting food. Whether you only scoop small portions onto a plate and get seconds later or just fill a child's glass half full of milk, there are hundreds of simple strategies to reduce food waste.

The best way to ensure that the leftovers in the refrigerator aren't going to fossilize is to conduct an inventory once a week. You can see what items need to be used up right away and which ones can go for a few more days. If you inventory the night before you grocery shop, you can use what you already have in some upcoming meals.

By using your imagination and following a few suggestions and tips, you can create some real assets to your pantry rather than tossing them in the garbage. Here are a few clever ideas to get you started on how to rescue almost-wasted foods:

Bananas—If the bananas are turning brown and you don't

have time to make banana bread or muffins, put them on ice. Bananas can be frozen whole in the skin. Simply thaw them out later for baking.

Broth—Whenever you cook vegetables in water, save the broth for later. A homemade stock is a great way to start a homemade soup or for cooking rice. Try keeping a covered container of vegetable stock in the refrigerator and add more to it each time you cook vegetables. When the container is full, plan on making soup the next day. The broth will taste better and is much healthier than canned broth with loads of sodium.

Vegetable blend—Don't throw out that last scoop or two of vegetables at the bottom of the serving bowl. Keep a covered container in the freezer for veggie bits. Once a week, add them to soups, stews or any recipe that calls for a vegetable medley.

Tomatoes—If the tomatoes are starting to get soft and wrinkly, you can toss them in a blender and use the fresh tomato sauce in a casserole or pasta dish. Or you can make your own sundried tomatoes. Slice them thin and layer them on waxed paper in a glass baking dish. Pour a little olive oil and balsamic vinegar over them, and then salt and pepper. Place the baking dish in a 300°F oven for about three hours. Remove and let the tomatoes cool. Store them in an airtight container in the refrigerator for a week or two and add this gourmet ingredient to any of your favorite recipes.

Potato chips—Never throw away the crushed chips at the bottom of the bag. Instead, pour them into a zippered plastic bag and crush them into a fine crumb mixture. This makes a great topping for casseroles or any recipe that calls for a bread crumb topping.

Crackers—Stale crackers won't go to waste when you crush them up and use them in meat loaf or meatballs instead of bread crumbs or oatmeal. Since crackers are usually salty, eliminate any salt in the recipe.

Stale bread—You'll never buy bread crumbs when you have stale bread on your hands. Just toss the bread in a blender or food processor and you'll have bread crumbs. Keep a container in the pantry and add to it. Use the bread ends, which many kids and adults just don't like to eat, for bread crumbs, too.

Harvest vegetables—When there are simply too many vegetables to handle, whether from your own garden or a neighbor's—turn to the freezer. Several veggies will keep their flavor, nutritional value and texture when frozen (such as green beans and peas), while others don't do well at all (potatoes, lettuce and celery). Many vegetables freeze well when chopped up and used later for stew or chili (tomatoes, peppers and onions). For convenience, blanch the vegetables (boil them in water for a few minutes), cool them, chop them and store in zippered freezer bags in ½-cup portions. Get creative and make blends, such as chopped green peppers and onions.

Citrus peels—Place these in a zippered bag in the freezer and pull them out when you need some lemon zest or orange zest. You can even grate them while frozen. It's a great way to add zing to an otherwise ordinary dish. Make sure you wash the outside well before using them this way.

The Well-Stocked Budget Pantry and Refrigerator

When planning for a wide range of meals, there are a number of items that a well-stocked budget pantry and refrigerator must include. This list is by no means inclusive and should be used as a starting point. However, this list does include grocery items that are traditionally inexpensive, store well and are versatile enough to appear in many different dishes without appearing bland or boring.

Remember, as long as you purchase an ingredient and get the most out of it, it is a wise purchase. If you absolutely love freshly grated Parmesan cheese, splurge and use it as a topping in as many meals as you can. If you consider walnuts to be the best thing ever, buy a bag and figure out ways to add them sparingly to meals.

Keep in mind which ingredients you use often and keep track of what needs to be replaced just before each shopping trip. If you see one of the must-have items on sale, stock up so you'll never pay full price again.

Try to keep these items in
your pantry:

» Biscuit baking mixes
» Bread
» Canned cream soups
» Canned tomatoes and
   tomato paste
» Canned vegetables
» Cereal
» Cheese
» Chips and crackers
» Condiments (ketchup,
   mustard, honey, etc.)
» Cornmeal
» Dry beans and canned
   beans
» Eggs
» Flour
» Frozen fruit and canned
   fruit
» Frozen mixed vegetables
» Lemon juice
» Margarine, shortening and
   cooking oil
» Meats (chicken, beef,
   pork, etc.)
» Milk
» Pasta
» Peanut butter
» Potatoes
» Rice
» Salt, pepper and spices
» Sugar (white, brown and
   powdered)
» Tuna

Chapter 4
Soups & Salads

Chili Macaroni Soup

Turn cheap boxed macaroni and cheese into a hearty meal for the whole hungry family.

$^1/_2$ **pound ground beef**
1 medium onion, chopped
$^1/_4$ **cup chopped green bell pepper**
5 cups water
1 (14-ounce) can diced tomatoes, undrained
1 (7$^1/_2$-ounce) package macaroni and cheese mix
$^1/_2$ **teaspoon chili powder**
$^1/_2$ **teaspoon garlic salt**
$^1/_4$ **teaspoon salt**
1 (8$^3/_4$-ounce) can corn, drained
2 tablespoons sliced black olives

In a large saucepan, cook beef, onion and bell pepper over medium heat until meat is no longer pink. Drain mixture, and then add water, tomatoes, cheese packet from mix, chili powder, garlic salt and salt. Simmer 10 minutes. Add pasta from mix, corn and olives. Cover and simmer 10 minutes or until macaroni is tender, stirring occasionally.

Serves 4–6

Top with sour cream and serve with tortilla chips.

Recipe Tip: **Cooked rice and cooked noodles are the perfect way to stretch a serving. Add a cup of cooked rice to a casserole or include a cup or two of cooked macaroni to a soup. Not only will they make the meal go further, but they'll add a serving from the bread and cereal food group.**

Corn Chowder

This is a perfect recipe for the slow cooker—just mix all ingredients together and cook on low 6 to 8 hours.

2½ cups milk
1 (14-ounce) can creamed corn
1 (10-ounce) can condensed cream of mushroom soup
1¾ cups frozen corn
1 cup frozen shredded hash brown potatoes
1 cup cubed cooked ham
1 onion, chopped
2 tablespoons margarine
½ teaspoon salt
¼ teaspoon pepper

Combine milk, creamed corn, soup and frozen corn in a large saucepan. Mix well, and then add potatoes, ham, onion, margarine, salt and pepper. Cover and cook over medium-low heat 30 minutes, or until heated through.

Serves 4–6

Serve in sourdough bread bowls.

Cheater Potato Soup

This soup is a wonderful way to use leftover vegetables. Simply add corn, carrots, peas or whatever you have on hand.

²/₃ cup margarine
¹/₂ cup minced onion
²/₃ cup flour
6 cups milk
4 to 6 large baking potatoes, baked and cooled
1 cup diced ham or 1 cup crumbled bacon
1 teaspoon garlic salt
1 cup sour cream
1 cup shredded cheddar cheese

In a large pot, melt margarine over medium-high heat and add onion. Cook until onion are translucent. Add flour and whisk in milk, stirring often about 4 to 6 minutes, or until thickened. In the meantime, cut potatoes lengthwise, scoop out whites and discard peels. Add potatoes, ham or bacon, and garlic salt. Stir gently to mix. Add sour cream and cheddar cheese and simmer on low 30 minutes.

Serves 4-6

Serve with breadsticks.

Bean Barley Soup

If you've never had barley before, this soup recipe will make you a fan, and soon you'll be adding it to other dishes.

2 (10-ounce) cans kidney beans, drained
1 pound precooked smoked sausage, thinly sliced
7 cups water or stock
1 cup barley, uncooked
½ onion, diced
Salt to taste

Place all ingredients in a slow cooker and cook 6 to 8 hours on low.

Serves 4–6

Serve with oyster crackers.

> ***Recipe Tip:*** **Dry beans are extremely inexpensive but require some advance preparation in order to use them. Simply measure the amount of beans required for the recipe and place in a container. Cover beans with cold water and cover with a lid. Set them aside for overnight, and the next day you'll have beans ready to be boiled.**

Bean and Ham Soup

To make a ham stock, place ham hocks and meaty bones in a saucepan with 2 quarts water. Then simmer over medium-low heat about 2 hours.

2 (10-ounce) cans white beans
1 cup chopped cooked ham
1 cup chopped onion
1 cup chopped celery
3 cups chopped raw potatoes
$3^1/_2$ cups vegetable stock, ham stock or water
$^1/_2$ teaspoon salt
$^1/_2$ teaspoon pepper

Combine all ingredients in a large saucepan and simmer over low heat 2 to $2^1/_2$ hours.

Serves 4–6

Serve with hot buttered cornbread.

Carrot Chowder

This soup freezes well, so double the recipe and put some away for a day when you don't have a lot of time.

1/2 pound ground beef, browned and drained
1/2 teaspoon salt
1/2 cup chopped celery
1/2 cup chopped onion
4 cups tomato sauce
1 1/2 cups water
2 1/2 cups grated carrots
1 teaspoon sugar
1/2 teaspoon garlic salt
1/2 teaspoon pepper
2 (10-ounce) cans condensed cream of celery soup

In a large saucepan, combine all ingredients except the condensed soup and mix well. Simmer about 30 minutes, or until carrots are tender. Add condensed soup and mix well. Simmer another 15 minutes.

Serves 4-6

Serve with a cucumber salad and fresh fruit on the side.

Hearty Orzo Chowder

Orzo, often called Rosa Marina or Rosa Seeds, is a small pasta that looks like rice.

1¼ cups uncooked orzo
5 slices bacon, diced
½ cup chopped onion
2 cups water
2 cups milk
1 (17-ounce) can creamed corn
Salt and pepper to taste

Cook orzo according to package directions; drain. Meanwhile, fry bacon in a large saucepan until crisp. Drain bacon, reserving 2 tablespoons of drippings; crumble and set aside. Return reserved drippings to pan and add onion, sautéing until tender. Add water, milk, corn and crumbled bacon and stir over medium heat until heated through, about 10 minutes. Stir in orzo and salt and pepper to taste.

Serves 4-6

Serve with toasted whole wheat bread and your favorite jam.

> *Recipe Tip:* When a recipe calls for crumbled bacon, don't just fry up the minimum amount. Instead, fry up the whole package, drain on paper towels and crumble. Store in an airtight container in the refrigerator for up to 10 days and use as needed.

Soups & Salads

Autumn Stew

When the gardens are bursting with vegetables, this hearty stew can handle any extra vegetables you want to throw in.

$^1/_4$ **cup flour**
1$^1/_2$ teaspoons salt
$^1/_4$ **teaspoon pepper**
1 pound beef stew meat, cut into 1-inch pieces
1 (16-ounce) can stewed tomatoes
2 cups water
$^1/_2$ **cup chopped onion**
1 clove garlic, finely chopped
2 beef bouillon cubes
3 medium potatoes, pared and cut into 1-inch cubes
2 cups cubed pumpkin or squash, cut into 1-inch cubes

Mix flour, salt and pepper together and coat meat with flour mixture. Brown meat in a saucepan over medium heat.* Stir in remaining ingredients except potatoes and pumpkin; heat to boiling. Reduce heat, then cover and simmer 20 minutes, or until meat is tender. Stir in potatoes and pumpkin, cover and simmer until vegetables are tender, about 30 minutes.

Serves 4–6

*To make this stew in a slow cooker, place browned meat in the bottom of the slow cooker and add the remaining ingredients on top. Cook on low about 6 hours and stir gently before serving.

Serve with hot buttered rolls and a green salad.

Mandarin Couscous Salad

Include a handful of toasted almonds to add an extra crunch to this versatile salad.

1¹/₃ cups water
1 cup uncooked couscous
1 (11-ounce) can mandarin oranges
1 cup frozen peas
¹/₃ cup chopped red onion
3 tablespoons white vinegar
2 tablespoons olive oil
1 tablespoon sugar
¹/₄ teaspoon salt
¹/₈ teaspoon pepper
¹/₄ teaspoon hot pepper sauce

Place water in a saucepan and bring to a boil. Add couscous; cover and remove from heat. Let covered saucepan stand 5 minutes, and then fluff couscous with a fork. Cover and refrigerate 1 hour. In a bowl, combine oranges, peas, onion and couscous. In a container with a tightly fitting lid, combine vinegar, oil, sugar, salt, pepper and hot pepper sauce, and shake well. Pour the dressing over the couscous mixture and toss to coat.

Serves 4-6

Serve with applesauce muffins:

Taco Pasta Salad

This is the kind of pasta salad that is made for substituting. Try different beans, such as black or kidney, use Colby Jack instead of cheddar and try green olives for black for a different south-of-the border taste every time.

1 package dry ranch dressing mix
1 package taco seasoning
1 (8-ounce) can corn, drained
1 (8-ounce) can pinto beans, drained
2 cups grated cheddar cheese
1 (8-ounce) can black olives, sliced
1 (16-ounce) bag corkscrew pasta, cooked and drained
15 to 20 tortilla chips, crushed, for garnish

Mix the ranch dressing according to package directions.

Mix the taco seasoning, corn, beans, cheese and olives together in a large mixing bowl. When combined thoroughly, add pasta and ranch dressing and mix to coat. Refrigerate at least 1 hour. Before serving, garnish with lightly crushed tortilla chips sprinkled on top.

Serves 4-6

Serve with cheese quesadilla wedges.

Asian Salad

A cup or two of cooked cubed chicken and a handful of almond slices can dress this salad up nicely.

1 small head lettuce
1 small head cabbage
¹/₂ cup mushroom pieces, drained
1 cup lightly crushed uncooked ramen noodles

Sauce:
³/₄ cup mayonnaise
2 tablespoons soy sauce
2 tablespoons sugar

Finely chop lettuce and cabbage and place in a large bowl. Add mushrooms and toss. Refrigerate 1 hour. Meanwhile, mix sauce and refrigerate. When ready to serve, toss salad with desired amount of sauce and add ramen noodles.

Serves 4-6

Serve with grilled teriyaki chicken wings.

Apple-Pineapple Coleslaw

Even those who don't usually like coleslaw find this
fruity combination irresistible.

1 (9-ounce) can pineapple tidbits, drained
1 cup diced, unpared apple
3 cups shredded cabbage

Sauce:
1 cup mayonnaise
¼ cup sugar
1 tablespoon vinegar
¼ teaspoon cinnamon

   Combine fruit and cabbage in a large bowl. Blend
dressing ingredients together and pour over cabbage
and fruit. Toss to coat well. Refrigerate 1 hour.

Serves 4-6

Serve with crusty bread and hot buttered green beans
topped with crumbled bacon.

Egg Salad

This makes a great sandwich spread as well as a salad.

4 hard-boiled eggs, peeled and chopped
1 celery stalk, finely chopped
1/4 cup light mayonnaise
1 1/2 teaspoons lemon juice
2 teaspoons finely chopped white onion
Salt and pepper to taste
4 lettuce leaves for serving

Gently toss the eggs and celery together in a medium-size bowl. In a smaller bowl, combine mayonnaise, lemon juice, onion, salt and pepper. Fold into the eggs and celery. Season to taste with salt and pepper. Chill 1 hour before eating. For each individual serving, spoon 1/2 cup salad onto a lettuce leaf or spread on bread.

Add one or two of these extras if you'd like:
» 6 green olives, chopped
» 1 tablespoon sweet pickle relish
» 2 tablespoons crumbled bacon
» 1 tablespoon finely chopped red, orange or yellow bell pepper
» 1 teaspoon prepared horseradish sauce
» 1 teaspoon prepared mustard
» 1 tablespoon Parmesan cheese

Serves 4–6

Serve with raw carrots and celery, and a creamy dip.

Easy Fruit Salad

Top with toasted shredded coconut before serving for a hint of the tropics.

1 cup mandarin orange slices, drained
1 cup chunk pineapple, drained
1 cup fruit cocktail, drained
1 cup small marshmallows, compacted
1 cup plain yogurt

Mix all ingredients together in a medium bowl and cover. Refrigerate overnight and stir before serving.

Serves 4-6

Serve with tuna fish sandwiches on whole wheat bread.

Cucumber Salad

This refrigerates well in a covered container for up to three days, so double the recipe and serve later in the week.

½ cup plain yogurt
1 tablespoon lemon juice
1 teaspoon sugar
1 teaspoon salt
Dash pepper
3 cups cucumber, halved lengthwise and thinly sliced
  (1 large cucumber)

Stir together yogurt, lemon juice, sugar, salt and pepper. Add cucumber slices and toss to coat. Cover and chill at least 2 hours, stirring occasionally. Stir before serving.

Serves 4–6

Serve with peppered pork chops and biscuits hot from the oven.

Chapter 5
Vegetable Dishes

Parmesan-Crusted Potatoes

Russet, red, Yukon gold—any kind of potato will do in this recipe.

8 medium potatoes
2 teaspoons margarine, melted
2 teaspoons lemon juice
¼ cup grated Parmesan cheese
½ teaspoon salt
¼ teaspoon pepper

Cut potatoes into quarters. In a bowl, combine margarine and lemon juice. In a separate bowl, combine cheese, salt and pepper. With a basting brush, brush cut surfaces of the potatoes with the margarine mixture, and then dip the coated sides into the cheese mixture. Place potatoes cut side up into a microwave-safe dish and cover. Microwave on high about 12 minutes, or until potatoes are tender.

Serves 4

Serve with a tossed green salad with fresh tomatoes and peas with golden honey wheat rolls.

Zucchini Cakes

When the farmers market, or your own garden, is full of zucchini, you can freeze shredded zucchini and enjoy this side dish year-round. Just be sure to dry the zucchini between paper towels after thawing.

3 cups shredded zucchini
1 egg, slightly beaten
2 tablespoons chopped onion
1 tablespoon margarine, melted
1 teaspoon mustard
1/2 teaspoon salt
1/4 teaspoon pepper
1 cup bread crumbs
1/4 cup vegetable oil

In a medium bowl, combine zucchini, egg, onion, margarine, mustard, salt and pepper. Mix well and shape into 6 small patties. Coat each patty with bread crumbs. Heat oil in a large skillet and fry patties 3 to 4 minutes on each side, or until golden. Remove patties from oil and drain.

Serves 4–6

Serve with mashed potatoes and mixed fruit salad.

Corny Bean Bake

Substitute broccoli for green beans if you like.

2 (15-ounce) cans green beans (any style), drained
1 (15¼-ounce) can corn, drained
1 (10¾-ounce) can condensed cream of mushroom soup
1 cup shredded cheddar cheese, divided
½ cup crushed butter-flavored crackers (about 10)

In a bowl, combine beans, corn, soup and ½ cup cheese. Pour into greased baking dish and top with remaining cheese and crackers. Bake uncovered at 350°F 30 minutes, or until heated throughout.

Serves 4

Serve with hot baked potatoes and hearty bran muffins.

Recipe Tip: **Cheese adds plenty of flavor to a dish, but since it's expensive, try reducing the amount the recipe calls for, especially when the recipe instructs you to "top with cheese."**

Sweet Potato Haystacks

For variety, use an ice cream scooper or a fun-shaped mold to form the sweet potatoes on the pineapple slice.

2 cups mashed canned sweet potatoes
1/2 cup packed brown sugar
2 tablespoons margarine
1/4 teaspoon salt
1/4 teaspoon ground cinnamon
1/4 teaspoon ground nutmeg
1 (20-ounce) can pineapple slices, drained

In a large bowl, combine sweet potatoes, brown sugar, margarine, salt, cinnamon and nutmeg. Place pineapple slices in a greased 9 x 13-inch baking dish. Top each slice with 1/4 cup sweet potato mixture. Bake uncovered at 400°F 15 minutes, or until heated through.

Serves 4–6

Serve with veggie-stuffed pita pockets drizzled with vinaigrette.

Corn Pone

This makes a lot of cornbread, so you can serve some for dinner and use the leftovers for another meal.

2 cups cornmeal
2/3 cup flour
1/4 cup sugar
4 teaspoons baking powder
1 1/2 teaspoons salt
1 teaspoon baking soda
4 eggs, beaten
2 cups milk
1 cup vegetable oil
1 small onion, finely chopped
2 (14 1/2-ounce) cans corn, drained

Combine cornmeal, flour, sugar, baking powder, salt and baking soda. Stir in eggs, milk, oil, onion and corn. Pour into a greased 9 x 13-inch baking dish. Bake at 400°F 30 minutes, or until a knife inserted in center comes out clean.

Serves 4-6

Serve with three bean salad and chilled melon slices.

Melon Boats

In late summer when the stores and farmers markets are overflowing with melons, try different combinations of melon, fruit and gelatin.

1 large melon (such as cantaloupe or honeydew)
2 (3-ounce) packages flavored gelatin
1 cup boiling water
½ cup applesauce
1 cup sliced fresh fruit

Cut melon in half lengthwise and scoop out seeds. Cut a thin slice off the bottom of the melon so the half will sit firm and level. In a bowl, dissolve gelatin in boiling water, then stir in the applesauce and fresh fruit. Pour gelatin mixture into the scooped-out center of the melon halves. Cover melons with plastic wrap and refrigerate overnight. Just before serving, slice melon halves into three wedges.

Serves 4–6

Try these gelatin and fruit combinations:
» Orange-flavored gelatin and chopped mandarin oranges
» Strawberry-banana-flavored gelatin and fresh strawberries
» Lemon-flavored gelatin and blueberries
» Lime-flavored gelatin and cubed, peeled apples
» Strawberry-flavored gelatin and sliced bananas

Serve with a hearty soup and warm breadsticks.

Baked Cabbage

A staple at the dinner table for decades, cabbage is making a comeback in tasty dishes such as this one.

1 large head cabbage
2 medium tomatoes, diced, or 1¹/₂ cups canned diced tomatoes, drained
1 small white onion, chopped
¹/₂ teaspoon garlic powder
¹/₂ teaspoon salt
1 teaspoon pepper
¹/₈ cup water, vegetable stock or chicken stock

Preheat oven to 325° F. Quarter the cabbage and boil in a large kettle 10 minutes. Remove cabbage quarters and place in a shallow baking dish. Combine remaining ingredients in a small bowl, and then pour over cabbage. Bake 30 minutes, or until liquid is absorbed. Turn cabbage pieces about halfway through cooking time so wedges cook evenly.

Serves 4

Serve with wide egg noodles in a creamy peppered cheese sauce.

> ***Recipe Tip:*** **A garden is a wonderful way to save money on vegetables. Start out small with a few tomato and pepper plants, and work your way up to a bountiful harvest. Make sure to freeze any excess.**

Sweet Potato Patties

Get canned sweet potatoes on sale or cook fresh sweet potatoes just as you would mashed potatoes— peel and boil.

3 cups cooked mashed sweet potatoes
1 tablespoon melted margarine
¹/₃ cup milk
¹/₂ teaspoon salt
1 teaspoon sugar
2 cups crushed corn flake cereal

Preheat oven to 325° F. Combine sweet potatoes, margarine, milk, salt and sugar. Form into 6 patties, and then roll in corn flakes to coat. Place on a greased baking sheet and bake 25 minutes.

Serves 4-6

Serve with grilled kebabs of cherry tomatoes, potatoes, peppers and squash on a bed of white rice.

Tomato Cakes

These must be cooked in shortening, not vegetable oil. Otherwise the tomato cakes will crumble while frying.

1 (15-ounce) can peeled tomatoes
1/2 medium onion, chopped fine
2 plastic packages saltine crackers
2 tablespoons shortening

Drain most, but not all, of the juice off the tomatoes, and then dice them in a bowl. Add chopped onion. Crumble crackers and stir into mixture until it has a stiff texture. Refrigerate half an hour so the crackers soften and soak up the liquid. Press mixture into 8 patties about 4 inches around. Fry in melted shortening in a skillet over medium-high heat about 4 minutes. Turn over halfway to brown on both sides.

Serves 4 (2 patties each)

Serve with baked beans and cornbread muffins.

Scalloped Potatoes

Add bread crumbs or crushed butter crackers in the last 5 minutes of baking for a crunchy topping.

¼ cup margarine
3 tablespoons flour
1 teaspoon salt
Dash pepper
3 cups milk
6 potatoes, peeled and thinly sliced

Preheat oven to 325°F. In a large saucepan over medium heat, melt margarine and whisk in flour, salt and pepper. When smooth, gradually add milk. Bring to a boil and stir constantly 3 minutes, until thickened. Place potato slices in a greased 9 x 9-inch baking dish. Add sauce and stir to coat. Cover and bake 30 minutes. Uncover and bake another 20 to 30 minutes, or until potatoes are tender.

Serves 4–6

Serve with summer squash or other in-season veggies.

Roasted Red Potatoes

If there are any leftovers, they make a flavorful addition to a soup or stew.

1 tablespoon Dijon mustard
1/4 cup vegetable oil
1/2 cup Parmesan cheese
1 tablespoon dried rosemary (optional)
1/4 teaspoon salt
1/4 teaspoon pepper
1/4 teaspoon garlic salt
10 red potatoes, quartered

Preheat oven to 400°F. In a large bowl, mix mustard, oil, cheese and spices together. Add the potatoes and toss to coat. Pour coated potatoes in an ungreased 9 x 13-inch baking dish. Bake, covered, 40 minutes, or until potatoes are tender.

Serves 4–6

Serve with tomato avocado sandwiches.

Recipe Tip: **Get more flavor from dried herbs by crushing them between your fingers. This releases the aromatic oils and intensifies the flavor.**

White Cheese Couscous

You can also substitute the same amount of instant grits for the couscous, resulting in a slightly different texture and taste.

5 cups water
1¹/₂ cups couscous
2 teaspoons salt
2 dashes hot sauce or ¹/₂ teaspoon cayenne pepper
¹/₄ cup margarine
¹/₂ cup shredded white cheese (not cheddar)
¹/₂ cup chopped mushrooms
3 eggs, beaten

Bring water to a rolling boil and stir in couscous, continuing to stir as needed 3 to 5 minutes, until thick. Remove from heat. Add salt, hot sauce or cayenne pepper, margarine, cheese, mushrooms and eggs. Mix well and place in a large ungreased baking dish. Bake uncovered at 275°F about 1 hour, or until heated through.

Serves 4-6

Serve with your favorite spicy entree and a side of tangy grapes.

Zucchini Boats

This also works well as a stuffed tomato recipe, using beefsteak tomatoes instead of zucchini.

4 medium zucchini
$1/2$ cup water
Salt
$1/2$ pound pork sausage
$1/4$ cup chopped onion
1 egg, slightly beaten
14 saltine crackers, finely crushed
$1/2$ cup shredded cheese
$1/4$ teaspoon salt
$1/8$ teaspoon garlic salt
$1/8$ teaspoon pepper
Paprika

Halve zucchini lengthwise. Scoop out pulp, leaving a $1/4$-inch-thick shell. Chop enough pulp to make 1 cup; set aside. Place zucchini shells, cut side down, in a large skillet. Add water, cover and simmer about 3 minutes, until tender. Drain. Remove zucchini from skillet and turn cut side up. Sprinkle with a little salt.

Heat oven to 350°F. In skillet, cook sausage and onion until meat is no longer pink and onion is tender; drain. Stir in reserved zucchini pulp, egg, cracker crumbs, cheese, salt, garlic salt and pepper. Mix well. Spoon mixture into zucchini shells. Place shells in a shallow baking pan and sprinkle with paprika. Bake, uncovered, about 25 minutes, or until heated through.

Serves 4–6

Serve with apple slices.

Sweet Potato Bake

The possibilities for sweet potatoes are endless—
they're nutritious and inexpensive.

3 cups sweet potatoes or yams, baked then mashed
2 eggs
1 teaspoon vanilla
1 cup sugar
$1/2$ cup margarine

Topping:
1 cup brown sugar
$1/2$ cup flour
$1/2$ cup margarine

Combine first 5 ingredients in a large bowl and mix
well. Pour in a 9 x 13-inch baking dish.

Mix topping ingredients well and sprinkle over
potato mixture. Bake at 350°F 30 minutes, or until
baked through.

Serves 4-6

*Serve with a leafy salad of lettuce, green peas, artichoke
hearts, diced bell pepper and crumbled blue cheese.*

Calico Beans

This is a fine dish for the stovetop or the slow cooker and provides plenty of leftover beans for other recipes. Add crumbled bacon or cooked sausage for extra kick.

1 (15-ounce) can butter beans, drained
2 (15-ounce) cans kidney beans, drained
1 (15-ounce) can black beans, drained
$1/3$ cup tomato sauce
$1/2$ cup barbecue sauce
2 tablespoons mustard
$1/3$ cup packed brown sugar
$1/3$ cup white sugar
1 teaspoon chili powder

Combine all ingredients and simmer in a saucepan over low heat 45 minutes. If using a slow cooker, cook on low 6 hours.

Serves 4-6

Serve with corn chips.

Tomato-Olive Couscous

This Mediterranean-inspired dish creates exotic flavor combinations from budget-friendly ingredients.

1 (14-ounce) can diced tomatoes, undrained
1/2 cup chopped onion
1/4 teaspoon pepper
1/8 teaspoon garlic powder
1 cup water
1/2 teaspoon salt
2/3 cup couscous
1/4 cup sliced black olives

In saucepan, combine undrained tomatoes, onion, pepper, garlic powder, water and salt. Bring to a boil, and then stir in couscous. Cover, remove from heat and let stand 5 minutes. Stir in olives and cover 2 minutes more.

Serves 4

Serve with bruschetta (bread topped with a slice of tomato and mozzarella drizzled with olive oil and baked).

Potatoes and Peas

If you can find a package of frozen peas and pearl onions on sale, use that in place of the peas and chopped onion.

8 small red potatoes, quartered (about 4 cups)
1 (10 3/4-ounce) can condensed cream of mushroom soup
1/3 cup milk
1/2 teaspoon crushed dried thyme leaves
1/8 teaspoon pepper
1/8 teaspoon lemon juice
1 (10-ounce) package frozen peas, thawed and drained
1/2 cup chopped onion

Place potatoes in a large saucepan and cover with water. Heat to boiling, and then reduce heat to medium. Cook 8 to 10 minutes, or until potatoes are fork-tender. Drain and set aside. In the same saucepan, combine soup, milk, spices and lemon juice, then mix thoroughly. Add potatoes, peas and onion. Over low heat, stir occasionally until onions cook and mixture is heated through.

Serves 4–6

Serve with stuffed green or red peppers.

Bean Toast

Add a little water for a softer consistency and use this hearty spread as a vegetable dip instead.

2 (15-ounce) cans garbanzo beans, drained
1 teaspoon olive oil
¼ teaspoon fresh ground pepper
4 to 6 slices bread
Parmesan cheese for topping

Preheat oven to 375°F. In a blender, mix garbanzo beans, oil and pepper until well blended. Meanwhile, place bread on a baking sheet. Spread bean mixture over bread and sprinkle cheese on top. Bake 7 to 9 minutes, or until bread is toasted and the bean spread is warmed.

Serves 4-6

Serve with a hearty tomato soup.

Black Bean Tacos

Grill the pepper and onions to add a fire-roasted flavor to these vegetarian tacos.

1 (10-ounce) can black beans, drained
1 clove garlic, minced
1 cup chopped zucchini or yellow summer squash
8 flour or corn tortillas
1 cup diced tomato
1 red pepper, sliced
1 onion, sliced
1½ cups shredded lettuce
½ cup shredded cheese, your choice

Place beans and garlic in a medium saucepan and cook on medium heat until warmed through. Stir in zucchini until mixed well and heated. Place a spoonful of bean-zucchini mixture onto a tortilla. Place tomato, pepper, onion, lettuce and cheese on top and wrap. Serve immediately.

Serves 4 (2 tacos each)

Serve with crispy corn chips and salsa.

Vegetable Lasagna

Feel free to add your own spices to this dish to give all those veggies a little zing.

$\frac{1}{2}$ **cup diced red pepper**
$\frac{1}{2}$ **cup diced green pepper**
$\frac{1}{2}$ **cup diced mushrooms**
$\frac{1}{2}$ **cup chopped onion**
1 tablespoon vegetable oil
1 (26-ounce) jar spaghetti sauce
2 cups small curd cottage cheese
12 oven-ready lasagna noodles
2 cups shredded cheese

Preheat the oven to 375°F. Saute peppers, mushrooms and onion in oil over medium heat until softened, about 3 minutes. Stir in spaghetti sauce and let simmer 10 minutes. Spoon about $\frac{1}{2}$ cup of sauce on the bottom of a 9 x 13-inch baking dish. Lay 4 lasagna noodles on the sauce. Top with $\frac{1}{3}$ of the cottage cheese, $\frac{1}{3}$ of the sauce mixture and $\frac{1}{3}$ of the shredded cheese. Repeat for two more layers. Cover with aluminum foil and bake 30 minutes. Remove the foil and continue baking for another 15 minutes until bubbling in the center. Let the lasagna rest 10 to 15 minutes before serving.

Serves 4-6

Serve with garlic bread and assorted olives.

Baked Polenta

Amazingly versatile, this northern Italian dish can be combined with other flavors for a different taste every time.

2 cups milk
2 cups chicken stock
1 cup yellow cornmeal
1 cup Parmesan cheese
2 cups spaghetti sauce
1/2 cup cooked spinach
1/2 cup diced tomatoes

Preheat oven to 350°F. In a large saucepan, combine milk and chicken stock, and bring to a boil over medium-high heat. Once mixture reaches a rolling boil, gradually whisk in cornmeal, making sure no lumps remain. Reduce heat to low and simmer, stirring constantly, until thick, about 5 minutes. Remove from heat and stir in cheese. Grease a 9 x 9-inch baking dish and pour in cornmeal mixture. Spread spaghetti sauce over the top, then sprinkle the spinach and tomatoes around evenly. Bake 20 to 30 minutes, or until sauce is bubbling in the center. Remove from oven and allow it to cool 15 minutes. Cut with a sharp knife and serve.

Serves 4-6

For variety, add some of these other toppings right after the tomato sauce:
  » Chunky vegetables in light oil
  » Roasted red bell peppers
  » Chopped fresh mushrooms
  » Fresh Parmesan cheese
  » Shredded cheese

Serve with stuffed manicotti.

Vegetable Dishes

Noodle Rice Pilaf

What a delicious way to use up the last handful of dry spaghetti noodles in a box.

¼ cup margarine
1 cup uncooked long grain rice
½ cup uncooked spaghetti noodles,
   broken into 1-inch pieces
2¾ cups chicken broth
½ cup sliced mushrooms
Salt and pepper to taste

In a saucepan, melt margarine over medium heat. Add the rice and noodles; cook and stir until lightly browned, about 4 minutes. Stir in broth and mushrooms and bring to a boil. Reduce heat and cover. Simmer 25 minutes, or until broth is absorbed and rice is tender. Remove from heat and let mixture sit 5 minutes, uncovered. Add salt and pepper, and stir before serving.

Serves 4

Serve with a sliced tomato and mozzarella cheese salad.

Tofu Burgers

Tofu is a nutritious and affordable replacement for meat, and this recipe is also kid friendly.

1 pound firm tofu
2 tablespoons minced green pepper
2 tablespoons minced onion
2 tablespoons vegetable oil
2 tablespoons chili powder
1 teaspoon prepared mustard
1 cup water
¼ cup catsup
2 teaspoons vinegar
2 teaspoons brown sugar
Salt and pepper to taste
4 hamburger buns

Mash tofu and mix with the green pepper and onion. Heat oil in a large frying pan, and then fry tofu with chili powder and veggies on high 5 to 7 minutes. Add remaining ingredients except buns, and then simmer 10 minutes. Serve on toasted buns.

Serves 4

Serve with a slice of your favorite cheese melted on top.

Caribbean Yam Casserole

This sweet tropical concoction is packed full of nutrients such as potassium, fiber, vitamins B1, B6 and C.

2 (16-ounce) cans yams, drained
2 medium bananas, thickly sliced
1/2 cup orange juice
1/2 teaspoon salt
1/8 teaspoon pepper
1/4 cup coarsely crushed corn flakes
2 tablespoons toasted flaked coconut

Preheat oven to 350 degrees. In a greased 9 x 13-inch casserole dish, arrange yams and bananas along the bottom. Pour juice over all, and then sprinkle with salt and pepper. Top with corn flakes and coconut. Bake, covered, 30 minutes.

Serves 4

Serve with a spicy jambalaya.

Chapter 6
Main Dishes

Cornbread Chicken

Make an extra big pan of cornbread earlier in the
week so there will be enough leftovers to add to this
tasty entree.

2 cups cubed cooked chicken
6 cups cubed cornbread
8 bread slices, cubed
1 medium onion, chopped
2 (10^3/$_4$-ounce) cans condensed cream of chicken soup
1 cup chicken broth or water
2 tablespoons margarine
1 teaspoon salt
^{1}/$_2$ teaspoon pepper

In a large bowl, combine all ingredients and gently
mix to coat chicken. Pour into a greased 9 x 13-inch
baking dish. Bake uncovered at 350°F 45 minutes, or
until heated through.

Serves 4–6

Serve with steamed asparagus.

> ***Recipe Tip:*** If a dish is lacking oomph, add
> some color by stirring in something extra.
> Try adding ^{1}/$_4$ cup of chopped items, such
> as peppers, pimientos, chiles, ripe olives,
> homemade sun-dried tomatoes or green
> onions. Even sprinkling some colorful herbs
> can liven up a dish.

Cream Cheese Chicken

House-brand cream cheese is great in this recipe.

2 tablespoons margarine
1 (8-ounce) package cream cheese, softened
1 (10.5-ounce) can condensed cream of chicken soup
¼ cup milk
Salt and pepper to taste
2 cups cooked cubed chicken
4 cups hot cooked rice

In a medium saucepan over medium heat, melt margarine and cream cheese. When thoroughly melted and blended, add soup and milk. Mix well and add salt and pepper to taste. Add chicken and simmer, uncovered, 15 minutes, or until mixture is hot and bubbly. Add a little milk if mixture becomes too thick. Serve over hot cooked rice.

Serves 4

Serve with hot rolls and coleslaw.

Swirled Chicken Sandwich

Use any combination of deli meat you prefer—ham, turkey, roast beef, pastrami and more.

1 (1-pound) loaf frozen bread dough, thawed
2 tablespoons margarine, softened
12 ounces thinly sliced deli meat
1/2 cup shredded cheddar cheese

On a lightly floured surface, roll dough into an 8 x 10-inch rectangle. Spread margarine over the rectangle, and then cover the dough with deli meat and cheese. Roll up the rectangle jellyroll style, starting with a long end. When rolled, pinch the seam to seal tightly. Tuck the dough ends under and place seam-side down on a greased baking sheet. Cover and let rise 20 minutes in a warm place. Bake at 350°F 25 minutes, or until golden brown. Remove from oven and let sit 5 minutes before slicing and serving.

Serves 4–6

Serve with wild rice soup.

> *Recipe Tip:* If there is a type of food that you simply must have but it doesn't fit into your budget, get creative. For example, if expensive cheese is your thing, but you can't justify the cost, try using it just in dishes where it's noticeable. Don't use the good stuff in mixtures and casseroles where a lesser cheese will do. Enjoy the fancy cheese where it is undisguised and will enhance the meal.

Savory Chicken

There's plenty of sauce in this creamy citrus dish.

8 pieces chicken (any combo of breast, thigh,
   wing, drumstick)
1 (10 ¾-ounce) can condensed cream of mushroom soup
1 cup orange juice
2 tablespoons dry onion soup mix

Place chicken in a greased 9 x 13-inch baking dish. Combine soup, juice and soup mix, and pour over chicken. Cover and bake at 350°F 45 minutes. Uncover and bake 15 minutes more.

Serves 4

Serve with mashed potatoes or rice.

Citrus Chicken

If you actually have any leftovers of this, it goes great in any number of recipes that call for 1 to 3 cups cubed chicken.

8 pieces chicken (any combo of breast, thigh, wing, drumstick)
1/2 cup melted margarine
1 (6-ounce) can frozen orange juice, thawed
1/4 cup honey
1/4 cup soy sauce

Pat chicken dry with paper towels and place in a 9 x 13-inch baking dish. In a medium saucepan over low heat, combine the margarine, orange juice, honey and soy sauce. Pour sauce over chicken. Cover with foil and bake slowly 1 1/2 hours at 325°F. Fresh orange slices can be used as garnish.

Serves 4–6

Serve with loaded baked potatoes and a garden-fresh green salad.

> *Recipe Tip:* **Make sure you are using the correct size dish that the recipe calls for. You'll have less mess because things won't boil over, and the ingredients will cook more completely when you use the right size container. Generally, 2 quarts = 8 x 8; 2 1/2 quarts = 9 x 9; and 3 quarts = 9 x 13.**

Chicken Rolls

This works with just about any kind of rounded roll, so don't forget to check out the day-old section of the bakery. Save the roll innards to make bread crumbs.

1 dozen dinner rolls
2 cups cooked cubed chicken
1 cup chopped mushrooms
1 (10³/₄-ounce) can condensed cream of chicken soup
1 cup mayonnaise
1 cup shredded cheddar cheese
Margarine for rolls

Preheat oven to 325°F. Cut off the tops of the dinner rolls (about ⅓ of the roll) and set tops aside. Gently pull out the inside of the rolls, leaving 12 mini bread bowls. Mix together the chicken, mushrooms, soup, mayonnaise and cheese. Spoon mixture into each bread bowl. Spread a thick layer of margarine on the cut side of the roll tops and place them on top of the filled roll. Bake, covered, 15 minutes, or until mixture is heated through.

Serves 4 (3 rolls each) or 6 (2 rolls each)

Serve with canned peaches and cream or a corn-and-peas medley.

Italian Mac Recipe

This makes enough for two meals, so eat one for dinner and freeze the second pan for later.

2 boxes macaroni and cheese mix
½ pound ground beef
1 small onion, diced
½ cup diced green bell pepper
1 (16-ounce) can meat-flavored spaghetti sauce
2 cups shredded mozzarella cheese

Preheat oven to 350°F. Make macaroni and cheese mixes according to package directions. Brown hamburger until no longer pink, and then drain. Add in onion and bell pepper, and cook together until tender. Drain and add spaghetti sauce. In a 9 x 13-inch baking dish, layer half the hamburger mixture, half the macaroni and half the mozzarella. Repeat layers, ending with the cheese on top. Bake uncovered until cheese bubbles in the center and mixture is heated through.

Serves 4–6 (two meals)

Serve with buttered broccoli.

Taco Casserole

This tastes wonderful without any toppings, but it's a smart way to use up any leftovers and sneak in a serving of vegetables.

1 pound ground beef
1 (15-ounce) package cornbread mix
1 (20-ounce) can refried beans
1 package taco seasoning
2 tablespoons water
1 cup shredded cheddar cheese

Optional toppings:
Shredded lettuce
Chopped tomato
Chopped onion
Sour cream, etc.

Preheat oven to 425°F. Brown ground beef until no longer pink, and then drain. Mix the cornbread batter according to the directions on the package, and then set aside. Mix refried beans, taco seasoning and water together in a medium bowl, and then spread beans on the bottom of a 9 x 13-inch baking dish. Add a layer of the ground beef and top with cheese. Pour cornbread batter over the cheese and bake 10 to 15 minutes, or until cornbread is done and a toothpick inserted into the center comes out clean. Garnish each serving with toppings, or serve plain.

Serves 4–6

Serve with butter-fried sliced plantains.

Cornbread Mexi-Pizza

This south-of-the-border meal can have mild or spicy taco flavoring.

1 (8-ounce) package corn muffin mix
1 pound ground beef
1 packet taco seasoning mix
1½ cups shredded cheddar cheese, divided

Preheat oven to 400°F. Prepare corn muffin mix as directed on package. Grease a 12-inch pizza pan and spread batter over it. Bake 10 minutes, or until cornbread is light brown. Meanwhile, brown meat until no longer pink and then drain. Add seasoning to beef and prepare as directed on package. Sprinkle 1 cup cheese over baked cornbread crust. Top with meat mixture and remaining cheese. Bake 5 minutes, or until cheese is melted and bubbly.

Serves 4–6

Serve with chopped tomato, shredded lettuce and salsa.

All In One Dish

Besides being economical, this meal makes cleanup a snap.

1 (15-ounce) can creamed corn
1 (10³/₄-ounce) can condensed tomato soup
5 potatoes, thinly sliced
¹/₂ pound ground beef, browned and drained
1 medium onion, diced
2 cups cooked macaroni

Preheat oven to 350°F. In a medium bowl, mix the creamed corn and soup together. Grease a large two-quart casserole dish and layer ingredients in this order: potatoes, ground beef, onion, macaroni and corn/soup mixture. Bake, uncovered, 30 minutes.

Serves 4

Serve with baked sweet potatoes.

> ***Recipe Tip:*** **When you cook more than you need for a recipe, you're saving time. For example, fry up all the ground beef you'll be using that week all at once. Simply use what you need that night and store the rest in an airtight container in the refrigerator. A few nights later when you need browned ground beef, you'll save time because you've already done it.**

Main Dishes

Ground Beef and Rice

This savory dish will have everyone begging for more and is sure to become a family favorite.

$1/2$ pound ground beef
$1/4$ cup chopped onion
1 ($10^3/4$-ounce) can condensed chicken noodle soup
1 ($10^3/4$-ounce) can condensed cream of mushroom soup
$10^3/4$ ounces water (simply fill the empty soup can)
$1/2$ cup uncooked rice

Preheat oven to 400°F. Brown meat and onion in a skillet until meat is no longer pink; drain. Add soups, water and rice to skillet and mix well. Pour into greased 9 x 9-inch baking dish and bake 1 hour, covered.

Serves 4

Serve with sautéed zucchini and squash.

Farmer's Strata

Use leftover mashed potatoes or instant—either way it'll taste wonderful.

8 cups mashed potatoes
1 (16-ounce) can corn, drained
1 (16-ounce) can creamed corn
1 pound ground beef, browned and drained
Salt and pepper to taste

Preheat oven to 350°F. Prepare mashed potatoes. Mix the corn together in a small bowl. In a 9 x 13-inch baking dish, layer the following: ⅓ of the mashed potatoes, ½ of the ground beef, ½ of the corn, ⅓ of the mashed potatoes, ½ of the ground beef, ½ of the corn and top with remaining mashed potatoes. Pat the potatoes with a spoon to form small peaks. Bake 30 minutes until potato peaks begin to brown and mixture is bubbling in the center.

Serves 4–6

Serve with sliced strawberries, bananas and apples.

Budget Meat Loaf

Finally, a meat loaf with ingredients that cost less yet that delivers the same homemade taste as the traditional version.

1 pound ground beef
1/2 pound ground pork
1 1/2 teaspoons salt
1/4 cup tomato sauce
3/4 cup milk
1 cup finely crushed corn flakes (or 1 cup dry bread crumbs)
1 egg
1 tablespoon dried onion flakes

Preheat oven to 325°F. Combine all ingredients in a large bowl and mix well. Shape into two loaves and place in bread pans. Bake 1 to 1½ hours, or until mixture is no longer pink in the center.

Serves 4–6

Serve with garlic mashed potatoes.

Mexican Haystacks

For a meaty version, just add a layer of cooked ground beef over the beans and top with cheese.

$^1/_2$ **onion, diced**
1 tablespoon margarine
1 (29-ounce) can refried beans
$^1/_2$ **cup water**
2 tablespoons taco seasoning
1 (6-ounce) can tomato sauce
6 cups cooked rice, any kind
2 cups shredded cheddar or Monterey Jack cheese
Sour cream (optional topping)

Sauté onion in margarine in a skillet over medium heat until translucent.

In another saucepan, warm the refried beans over medium heat 8 to 10 minutes. Add the water and the taco seasoning. Add tomato sauce and stir until mixed thoroughly.

To serve: Place 1 cup cooked rice onto each person's plate. Layer approximately $^1/_2$ cup bean mixture over the rice and layer onions on top. Top with grated cheese and sour cream.

Serves 4-6

Serve with a fruit smoothie.

Fake Steak

This is more tender and has better flavor than any cubed steak.

Steaks:
1 pound ground beef
1¹/₂ cups bread crumbs
¹/₂ cup milk
1 egg
¹/₂ package dry onion soup mix
Flour

Sauce:
1 (10³/₄-ounce) can condensed cream of mushroom soup
1 cup milk
¹/₂ package dry onion soup mix
¹/₂ cup sliced mushrooms

Combine steak ingredients except flour, and mix well. Press into a 7 x 12-inch pan. Chill 30 minutes to 1 hour. Cut meat into 6 pieces. Coat each piece with flour and brown in a nonstick pan. Place coated pieces into a 9 x 13-inch baking pan.

To make the sauce, mix soup and milk. Add the dry onion soup mix and mushrooms. Pour over meat and cover with foil. Bake 1 hour at 350°F.

Serves 4–6

Serve with mashed potatoes or rice.

Cabbage Tomato Rolls

These are elegant enough to serve at a dinner party and nobody will ever guess they cost pennies per serving.

1 large head cabbage
1/2 pound lean ground beef
1/2 cup cooked rice
1 egg, lightly beaten
1/2 cup finely chopped onion
1/2 teaspoon salt
1/8 teaspoon pepper
1 teaspoon cinnamon (more or less, to taste), divided
1 (10 1/2-ounce) can condensed tomato soup
1 (14 1/2-ounce) can tomatoes

Tear the leaves off the cabbage and cook in boiling water or steam until wilted enough to be flexible. Cool. Mix ground beef, rice, egg, onion, salt, pepper and 1/2 teaspoon cinnamon together. Scoop a few tablespoons of the mixture into the center of a cabbage leaf, and then roll up in the leaf. Secure the stuffed cabbage rolls with toothpicks and place them in a 9 x 13-inch baking dish. Combine the soup and tomatoes and pour over cabbage rolls. Sprinkle with about 1/2 teaspoon of cinnamon. Cover and bake 1 hour, or until the cabbage rolls are cooked through.

Serves 4–6

Serve with potato wedges.

Budget Stroganoff

Substitute ground beef with leftover roast beef, shredded beef or even stew meat in 1-inch cubes.

½ pound ground beef
2 tablespoons dry onion soup mix
1½ cups water
2 tablespoons cornstarch
1 cup plain yogurt
4 cups cooked egg noodles

Brown beef in a large skillet, and then stir in soup mix and water. Cover and simmer 10 minutes. Combine cornstarch and yogurt, and then stir into meat mixture. Heat thoroughly but do not allow mixture to boil. Serve stroganoff over hot noodles.

Serves 4

Serve with corn on the cob or buttered corn niblets.

Recipe Tip: Whenever a recipe calls for sour cream, substitute plain yogurt, cup for cup. The taste difference is negligible and the savings are big.

Tuna Patties

Keep these ingredients on hand and you've got a classic go-to meal for when you haven't planned anything at all.

2 (6-ounce) cans tuna, well drained
1 egg
8 crackers, crushed (salted or butter)
1 teaspoon soy sauce
Garlic powder to taste
Salt and pepper to taste
$1/2$ to 1 cup vegetable oil, for frying
4 hamburger buns

Mix tuna, egg, cracker crumbs, soy sauce and spices until combined. Mixture should be moist but firm enough to hold together. Add more crushed crackers if mixture is too moist.

Form 4 patties. Heat oil in a skillet over medium-high heat. Place patties in skillet and cook on each side until golden (about 4 minutes on each side). Drain patties on paper towels. Serve patties on hamburger buns. Serve with sliced cheese, sliced tomatoes and lettuce.

Serves 4

Serve with fruit cocktail and carrot sticks and dip.

Tuna Barbecue

There is no trace of tuna flavor—it tastes just like a tender roast.

3 (6-ounce) cans tuna in water, well drained
¼ cup finely diced yellow onion
¼ cup finely diced green bell pepper
1½ cups barbecue sauce
4 hamburger buns, lightly toasted
4 slices of your favorite cheese for topping, optional

Combine all ingredients except buns and cheese in a nonstick skillet over medium-high heat, stirring occasionally. Heat thoroughly about 10 to 15 minutes. Scoop mixture onto toasted buns and top with cheese.

Serves 4

Serve with potato salad.

Fish Stick Casserole

Watch the supermarkets for frozen food sales and stock up on fish sticks.

1 (14-ounce) package frozen breaded fish sticks
2 tablespoons lemon juice
1 cup plain yogurt
1½ cups processed cheese, shredded or finely diced
¼ cup milk
1 tablespoon dry onion soup mix
1 teaspoon salt
¼ teaspoon pepper
4 medium potatoes, baked and thinly sliced
3 slices bacon, cooked and crumbled

Preheat oven to 450°F. Arrange fish sticks on a baking sheet and bake until they are just crisp, about 15 minutes. Reduce oven temperature to 350°F. Meanwhile, mix lemon juice, yogurt, cheese, milk, soup mix, salt and pepper in a medium bowl. Fold in potato slices and gently coat potatoes.

Place fish sticks upright around the inner edge of a greased 1½-quart casserole dish. Turn potato mixture into casserole dish and sprinkle with bacon. Cover loosely with foil and bake 25 minutes. Remove foil and bake until potato mixture is bubbly and fish sticks are golden brown, about 20 minutes.

Serves 4–6

Serve with a fresh spinach salad.

Tuna Boats

Made with some of the least expensive ingredients on the market, these fun and filling hot sandwiches are the ultimate inexpensive meal.

2 (6-ounce) cans tuna in water, well drained
2 tablespoons pickle relish
3 hard-boiled eggs, peeled and chopped
½ cup mayonnaise
½ cup shredded cheese, your choice
Salt and pepper to taste
4 hot dog buns

Preheat oven to 350°F. Combine tuna, relish, eggs, mayonnaise, cheese and seasoning; mix well. Place mixture onto the hot dog buns. Wrap each bun in foil and bake 15 minutes, or until warmed through.

Serves 4

Serve with blue corn chips and salsa.

Creamy Tuna Noodles

The traditional tuna noodle casserole gets a budget makeover with delicious results.

6 cups cooked egg noodles
2 (6$^1/_8$-ounce) cans tuna in water, drained well
$^1/_2$ cup canned mushrooms
1 cup frozen corn, thawed
1$^1/_2$ cups plain yogurt or sour cream
$^3/_4$ cup milk
1 green onion, chopped
$^1/_4$ teaspoon salt
$^1/_4$ teaspoon pepper
$^1/_4$ cup dry bread crumbs
$^1/_4$ cup grated cheddar cheese
2 tablespoons margarine, melted

Preheat oven to 350°F. In a medium bowl, mix noodles, tuna, mushrooms, corn, yogurt, milk, onion, salt and pepper. Pour mixture in an ungreased 9 x 9-inch baking dish. In a separate bowl, mix bread crumbs, cheese and margarine together, and then sprinkle over tuna mixture. Bake, uncovered, 35 minutes, or until mixture is bubbly.

Serves 4–6

Serve with buttered peas.

Asian Ham Topper

If you don't have any ham on hand, substitute 1
(16-ounce) can tuna, well drained, or 1 cup cooked
diced chicken.

1 (10-ounce) bag frozen Asian-style vegetables, thawed
1 (10 3/4-ounce) can condensed cream of mushroom soup
2 cups cooked diced ham
3/4 cup diagonal slices celery
1 tablespoon soy sauce
1/4 teaspoon pepper
3/4 cup crumbled uncooked ramen noodles

Preheat oven to 350°F. Mix all ingredients except
noodles into an ungreased casserole dish. Bake,
uncovered, 40 minutes, or until mixture is bubbly,
and then top with noodles. Bake an additional 5 minutes, or until noodles begin to brown.

Serves 4

Serve over hot rice, a baked potato or toast.

Stovetop Ham and Potatoes

If you don't have cooked potatoes on hand, chop up raw potatoes and lightly fry them in oil. When tender, add the other ingredients.

4 cups cubed cooked, peeled potatoes
2 cups diced cooked ham
$1/2$ cup mayonnaise or salad dressing
$1/4$ teaspoon salt
$1/8$ teaspoon pepper
1 cup shredded cheese, your choice

In a large skillet, combine potatoes, ham, mayonnaise, salt and pepper. Cook over medium-low heat until heated through, stirring occasionally. Stir in cheese until melted. Serve immediately.

Serves 4

Serve with a green-bean-and-sliced-mushroom blend, sprinkled with almonds.

Broccoli Ham Rollups

These can be frozen for several weeks as long as they are covered in double foil.

1 (10-ounce) package frozen broccoli
1 (10³/₄-ounce) can condensed cream of mushroom soup
1 cup dry bread crumbs
¹/₄ cup shredded cheddar cheese
1 tablespoon chopped onion
¹/₈ teaspoon dried crushed rosemary
¹/₈ teaspoon pepper
12 slices fully cooked ham (about ¹/₈-inch thick)

Preheat oven to 350°F. Cook broccoli according to package directions; drain and chop. In a medium bowl, combine soup, bread crumbs, cheese, onion and seasonings. Add broccoli; mix well. Spoon ¼ cup of the broccoli mixture onto each ham slice; roll up. Place rolled ham slice in an ungreased 9 x 13-inch baking dish. Cover with foil and bake 35 minutes, or until heated through.

Serves 4 (3 ham rolls each) or 6 (2 ham rolls each)

Serve with fresh fruit in a creamy yogurt sauce.

Recipe Tip: **Grow your own herb garden for pennies. There are many herb-growing kits available or make your own. Seeds can be purchased at any home and garden center. Nothing livens up a dish like fresh herbs.**

Pork Stir-Fry with Spicy Peanut Sauce

Get all the great taste of Thai food without the restaurant price.

1/2 cup creamy or chunky peanut butter
1/2 cup water
2 tablespoons soy sauce
1 tablespoon brown sugar
2 tablespoons vegetable oil
2 to 3 cloves garlic, minced
1/2 cup diced onion
2 cups diced cooked pork or shredded pork
3 to 4 cups sliced broccoli
4 cups hot cooked rice

In a small bowl, blend peanut butter, water, soy sauce and sugar, and then set aside. In a wok or large skillet, heat oil over high heat. Add garlic and onion, and stir-fry 30 seconds. Add pork and broccoli, and stir-fry about 3 to 5 minutes, or until broccoli is bright green. Stir in peanut butter mixture and cook, stirring constantly, until sauce is smooth, about 3 minutes. Serve over hot rice.

Serves 4

Serve with spring rolls or fried won ton crisps.

Orange Pork Chops and Rice

This recipe would allow the substitution of chicken breasts for the pork chops with no problem.

4 tablespoons margarine
6 pork chops, with or without bone
1 cup uncooked instant rice
2 cups orange juice or orange-flavored breakfast drink
2 (10³/₄-ounce) cans condensed cream of chicken soup
1 teaspoon salt
¹/₄ teaspoon pepper

In a large skillet, melt margarine and brown chops on both sides, about 4 minutes. Remove meat and add uncooked rice. Stir to coat rice well and then remove from heat. Combine all ingredients in a slow cooker and lay browned chops on top. Cover with lid and cook on high 3 to 4 hours.

Serves 4–6

Serve with steamed oriental vegetables.

Ham and Cheese Potatoes

This cheesy sauce also works well when served over hot cooked rice.

3 medium baking potatoes, baked
1 cup diced processed cheese
¼ cup milk
1 tablespoon mustard
½ teaspoon pepper
2 cups cubed cooked ham
1 cup frozen or canned peas

   While potatoes are cooling, combine cheese and milk in a saucepan over medium heat until smooth. Add mustard and pepper, stirring occasionally until cheese melts completely, and then add ham and peas. Reduce heat to low and stir occasionally until heated through, about 5 minutes. Cut potatoes in half lengthwise and spoon sauce over each half.

Serves 4–6

Serve with three bean salad.

Curry Pork with Apples

If your family doesn't like the taste of curry, substitute the same amount of dry onion soup mix.

1 tablespoon vegetable oil
$\frac{1}{2}$ pound lean pork, diced
2 apples, peeled, cored and chopped
$\frac{1}{2}$ cup chopped onion
2 tablespoons flour
1 teaspoon curry powder
$\frac{1}{4}$ teaspoon salt
$\frac{1}{4}$ teaspoon garlic powder
2 cups chicken broth
1 tablespoon lemon juice
1 ($1\frac{1}{2}$-ounce) box raisins (snack size)
4 cups hot cooked rice

In a large skillet, heat oil over medium heat. Brown the diced pork. Add apples and onions; brown lightly. Add flour and curry powder, and stir to blend well. Stir in remaining ingredients and cover. Simmer 35 to 45 minutes. Serve over hot cooked rice.

Serves 4

Serve with baked eggplant or potato slices seasoned with garlic, pepper and oil.

> ***Recipe Tip:*** When a recipe calls for cooked rice, look beyond the pale. Substitute cup for cup with something else, such as brown rice, couscous or other rices that you can find at ethnic food stores for very little money.

Pork Loaves

A fine alternative to meat loaf, this recipe makes two loaves.

3 pounds ground pork
1 (8 ounce) can tomato sauce
1 egg
¼ cup finely chopped green bell pepper
2 teaspoons salt
2 teaspoons chili powder
⅛ teaspoon pepper
6 cups prepared cornbread stuffing*
2 tablespoons ketchup

Combine pork, tomato sauce, egg, bell pepper and seasonings. Pat out half of the mixture onto wax paper and form an 8 x 10-inch rectangle. Place half the stuffing in a layer over meat, pressing lightly. Rolling from the short end in jellyroll fashion, roll the meat up to form a loaf. Seal ends and place seam-side down on a rack in roasting pan. Bake 1 hour. Spread ketchup on top and bake 15 minutes more. Prepare second loaf and wrap in plastic, and then foil. Store in freezer 2 to 3 weeks.

Makes 2 loaves, 4–6 servings each

*You can find inexpensive cornbread stuffing mixes at the grocery store. Prepare as directed on the box.

Serve with pasta salad.

Stuffed Pork Chops

Pair this filling main dish with mountains of rice or mashed potatoes—a great way to use up the creamy gravy.

1/2 cup chopped celery
1/2 cup chopped onion
4 tablespoons margarine, divided
1 cup seasoned stuffing croutons
6 tablespoons milk
1/4 teaspoon salt
1/4 teaspoon pepper
4 boneless pork loin chops (about 1 inch thick)
1 1/2 cups broth (chicken or vegetable)
2 tablespoons cornstarch
4 tablespoons cold water

Preheat oven to 350°F. In a skillet, sauté celery and onion in 2 tablespoons margarine until tender. Transfer to a medium bowl. Add croutons, milk, salt and pepper, and mix well. Cut a pocket in each pork chop and fill with stuffing.

In a skillet, brown chops in remaining margarine and transfer to a greased 9 x 9-inch baking dish. Pour broth into dish, and then cover and bake 35 minutes. Remove chops and keep warm.

For gravy, pour the pan drippings into a saucepan and bring to a boil. Combine cornstarch and water until smooth, and gradually stir into drippings. Cook and stir 2 minutes, or until thickened. Serve with pork chops.

Serves 4

Serve with steamed vegetables and hot buttered rolls.

Ziti and Sausage

So much fancier than plain old spaghetti, ziti is a macaroni almost 2 inches long.

3 cups cooked ziti
1/2 pound sweet Italian sausage or other link sausage cut
    into 1/4-inch slices
1/2 cup diced green bell pepper
1 (32-ounce) jar spaghetti sauce
1/2 cup water

   Cook ziti according to package directions. Meanwhile, brown sausage and bell pepper in a large saucepan. Cover and cook over medium-low heat 15 minutes; drain excess liquid. Pour in spaghetti sauce and water and heat through. Stir in ziti and serve.

Serves 4–6

Serve with eggplant Parmesan.

Spaghetti Pie

Instead of plain old spaghetti, bake this unusual Italian-flavored pasta dish.

1 (10-ounce) package uncooked spaghetti noodles
1/4 cup margarine, softened
1/2 pound Italian sausage
1 small onion, chopped
1/2 cup chopped mushrooms
1/2 cup chopped red or green bell pepper
1/2 teaspoon dried oregano
1/2 teaspoon salt
2 eggs, slightly beaten
1 cup shredded cheese, your choice

Preheat oven to 375°F. Grease a 10-inch glass pie dish and dust with flour. Cook spaghetti as directed on the package; drain. Toss cooked noodles with margarine and set aside. Cook the sausage, onion, mushrooms and bell pepper in a skillet over medium heat, stirring frequently, until sausage is no longer pink; drain. Toss spaghetti, sausage mixture, spices and eggs together, and pour into prepared pie dish. Sprinkle with cheese and cover with foil. Bake 45 minutes, or until hot. Cut into wedges and serve.

Serves 4–6

Serve with steamed broccoli and cauliflower.

Breakfast Casserole

Overall, breakfast food is pretty inexpensive, so consider adding this and other filling breakfast favorites into the dinnertime rotation.

$^1/_2$ **pound ground sausage, browned and drained**
$^3/_4$ **cup milk**
$^1/_4$ **cup melted margarine**
9 large eggs, slightly beaten
1 (24-ounce) package hash browns
1 cup shredded cheddar cheese

Preheat oven to 350°F. Layer sausage on the bottom of a well-greased 9 x 13-inch pan. Add milk and margarine to beaten eggs and pour mixture over sausage. Layer hash browns on top and sprinkle with cheese. Bake 1 hour, covered.

Serves 4–6

Serve with sliced cantaloupe.

> **Recipe Tip:** Substitute traditional cheese with some processed cheese whenever you can, especially when it comes to topping a casserole. Processed cheese is a blend of pasteurized cheeses with less fat and more moisture—yet costs significantly less than most cheeses. Just melt a few slices on top for an irresistible finishing touch.

Puffed Pancake with Sausage

Everyone's happy when it's "breakfast for dinner" night using inexpensive ingredients.

1 (8-ounce) package brown-and-serve sausage links
2 eggs, beaten
1 cup milk
1 tablespoon cooking oil
1 cup flour
¼ teaspoon salt

Grease the bottom and 1 inch up the sides of a 9 x 9-inch baking dish. Set aside. Slice sausage into small pieces and brown in a large skillet; drain. Meanwhile, in a medium bowl, combine eggs, milk and oil; stir in flour and salt. Beat until smooth and then pour batter into greased baking dish. Sprinkle sausage pieces into batter. Bake 35 minutes, or until puffed and golden brown. Serve immediately with syrup or honey.

Serves 4

Serve with hash browns.

Cabbage and Brats

Put a new face on these everyday foods by combining them in an irresistible blend of flavors.

1 small head cabbage (1½ pounds)
1 large sweet onion
4 links turkey bratwurst, cut into 1-inch pieces
2 tablespoons soy sauce
¾ teaspoon garlic powder
½ teaspoon pepper

Cut cabbage in half through the core. Remove core and cut cabbage into ¼-inch slices; set aside. Cut onion into ¼-inch slices; set aside. In a large nonstick skillet coated with cooking spray, cook and stir bratwurst pieces over medium-high heat 8 to 10 minutes, or until browned on all sides. Drain and set aside and keep warm. Add cabbage and onions to the same skillet. Cook and stir 6 minutes. Sprinkle with soy sauce, garlic powder and pepper. Cook and stir 4 minutes more. Return bratwurst to skillet and cook 2 minutes. Cover and reduce heat; simmer 5 minutes more, or until veggies are tender and brats are cooked through. Serve immediately.

Serves 4

Serve with cheesy scalloped potatoes.

Steak Strips

Check the butcher's markdown shelf for some great cuts of steak at rock-bottom prices.

⅓ cup flour
1 teaspoon salt
1 teaspoon pepper
½ pound steak (your choice of cut), sliced into
  ¼-inch strips
½ onion, sliced
1 (16-ounce) can tomatoes
1 (4-ounce) can mushrooms
3 tablespoons soy sauce
1 (10-ounce) can cut green beans

Mix flour, salt and pepper together in a shallow dish. Coat steak strips in flour mixture and place in the bottom of a greased slow cooker. Add all other ingredients except green beans on top. Cook on low 6 hours. About 40 minutes before serving, add green beans and stir to combine.

Serves 4–6

Serve with hot brown rice.

Saucy Steak

This is a good recipe for cheaper cuts of steak because the intense flavor and slow cooking make them savory and tender.

1 (8-ounce) can tomato sauce
$\frac{1}{2}$ teaspoon salt
2 tablespoons brown sugar
$\frac{1}{4}$ teaspoon vinegar
$\frac{1}{4}$ teaspoon barbecue sauce
$\frac{1}{4}$ cup flour
$1\frac{1}{2}$ pounds beef round steak, $\frac{1}{2}$ inch thick
Salt and pepper to taste
1 onion, sliced

Preheat oven to 350°F. In a medium bowl, mix tomato sauce, salt, sugar, vinegar, barbecue sauce and flour until smooth. Pour half the tomato mixture into a greased 9 x 13-inch baking dish. Place meat on the sauce and season with salt and pepper. Spread remaining tomato mixture over meat and top with onion slices. Cover dish securely with foil and bake $1\frac{1}{2}$ hours, or until tender. Slice steak into 4 servings.

Serves 4

Serve with baked potatoes and wheat rolls.

Slow Cooker Pot Roast with Vegetables

Although a roast may seem expensive, it can contribute to two or three meals. For example, try thin slices of leftover roast in a stir-fry or shredded in burritos.

4 pounds beef chuck pot roast
1 tablespoon vegetable oil
1 teaspoon salt
1/4 teaspoon pepper
1 clove garlic, crushed
5 medium carrots, cut into 2-inch pieces
4 medium potatoes, quartered
2 stalks celery, cut into 1-inch pieces
1 green bell pepper, cut into 1-inch pieces
1/4 cup apple juice
1/4 cup water

Trim excess fat from meat. Brown meat in oil about 10 minutes in a medium skillet over medium heat. Sprinkle with salt, pepper and garlic, and place in a slow cooker. Place vegetables around meat, and then add apple juice and water. Cover and cook about 6 hours on low.

Serves 4–6

Serve with blueberry muffins.

Confetti Hash

Exchange the corned beef for cooked ground beef or even diced ham.

2 tablespoons margarine
1¹/₂ cups cooked corned beef
¹/₂ cup finely chopped onion
¹/₄ teaspoon dried thyme
2 medium potatoes, cooked and chopped (about 2 cups)
1 small bell pepper, chopped (about ¹/₂ cup)
2 hard-boiled eggs, chopped

Heat margarine in a nonstick skillet over medium heat. Stir in all ingredients and cook, uncovered, 8 to 10 minutes, stirring frequently, until mixture is hot.

Serves 4

Serve with buttered toast and a leafy green salad with sliced berries and a berry vinaigrette.

> ***Recipe Tip:*** **Check out ethnic shops for great deals on spices. If you do have to purchase spices at the supermarket, try buying one small bottle every other week. After a few months, you'll have a nice assortment of must-have spices. Start with thyme, oregano, garlic powder and pepper, and branch out from there.**

Corned Beef and Eggs

A quick and filling meal for breakfast, lunch or dinner.

Creamy Mustard Sauce
1 cup plain yogurt
1/4 cup prepared mustard
1/4 teaspoon pepper
1 to 2 teaspoons milk
2 (15-ounce) cans corned beef hash
1/2 cup bread crumbs
1/2 teaspoon pepper
1 teaspoon vegetable oil
4 eggs, poached
Salt and pepper to taste
4 pieces bread, toasted

In a small saucepan over medium-low heat, mix yogurt, mustard, pepper and milk, stirring until blended. Stir occasionally, 3 to 5 minutes, or until heated through. Add milk as necessary to get the right consistency. Makes 1 cup (four 1/4-cup servings).

In a medium-size bowl, mix corned-beef hash and bread crumbs with pepper. Flatten mixture out between 2 pieces of waxed paper to about 1-inch thick. Cut into 12 large circles.* In a hot skillet, brown circles in oil on both sides. Top each circle with a poached egg and sprinkle with salt and pepper. Serve on buttered toast with creamy mustard sauce.

Serves 4

*Circles can be formed ahead of time and refrigerated until ready to cook.

Serve with fresh fruit.

Turkey Manicotti

Usually full of expensive cheeses, this stuffed manicotti recipe has been revised to use low-cost ingredients with delicious results.

1 pound ground turkey
1/2 cup finely chopped onion
1/2 teaspoon salt
1/4 teaspoon pepper
1 (8-ounce) package cream cheese
1 tablespoon milk
1 cup frozen chopped spinach, thawed and squeezed dry
1/4 cup Parmesan cheese
1 egg
4 cups prepared spaghetti sauce
8 cooked manicotti shells, drained and cooled
1/2 cup grated cheese, your choice

Preheat oven to 350°F. In a medium skillet over medium heat, combine turkey, onion, salt and pepper. Stir occasionally and cook until turkey is no longer pink, breaking up ground turkey halfway through cooking time, about 8 minutes. In a large bowl combine cream cheese, milk, spinach, Parmesan and egg. Mix until smooth and then add turkey mixture. Stuff each shell with approximately 1/2 to 3/4 cup turkey mixture. Spoon 2 cups spaghetti sauce into the bottom of a 9 x 13-inch baking dish. Layer shells over sauce. Top shells with any remaining turkey mixture and spaghetti sauce. Cover and bake 35 minutes, or until heated through. Sprinkle cheese over top and bake, uncovered, 5 minutes more. Let stand 15 minutes before serving.

Serves 4

Serve with crusty bread and a tossed salad.

Turkey Shepherd's Pie

A great recipe for using leftover meat—try ground beef or diced ham instead of ground turkey.

1 pound ground turkey
1 onion, chopped
2 tablespoons oil
3 cups spaghetti sauce
2 cups frozen mixed vegetables, thawed
Salt and pepper to taste
6 cups mashed potatoes, instant or traditional
2 tablespoons margarine, softened

Preheat oven to 350°F. In a medium skillet over medium heat, cook turkey and onion in oil until turkey is no longer pink; drain. In a medium bowl, combine turkey mixture, tomato sauce, vegetables and salt and pepper to taste. Stir to combine and pour into greased 9 x 13-inch baking dish. Spread out evenly and then top with mashed potatoes. Spread potatoes until turkey mixture is completely covered. Cover with foil and bake 25 minutes, or until mixture is bubbly. To serve, spread margarine over the mixture.

Serves 4-6

Serve with sautéed red and green pepper slices, drizzled with balsamic vinegar.

White Chili with Turkey

A mild version of traditional chili, this makes plenty for leftovers.

2 cups cubed cooked turkey breast or cooked ground turkey
3 (15-ounce) cans Northern (or other white) beans, rinsed and drained
1 (10^3/$_4$-ounce) can condensed cream of chicken soup
1^1/$_3$ cups milk
1 tablespoon dried minced onion
1 teaspoon garlic powder
1 teaspoon dried oregano
6 tablespoons sour cream

In a large saucepan, combine all ingredients except sour cream over medium heat. Cover and let simmer 30 minutes, or until heated through. Garnish with sour cream.

Serves 4–6

Serve with warm buttered tortilla wedges for dipping.

Enchilada Casserole

Here's one dish that tastes wonderful when heated in the microwave as tomorrow's lunch.

1 pound ground turkey
1 small onion, chopped
1 tablespoon plus ⅓ cup vegetable oil, divided
⅓ cup flour
2 tablespoons chili powder
¼ teaspoon salt
¼ teaspoon pepper
2 cups water
12 (7-inch) corn tortillas
1½ cups salsa
1½ cups of your favorite shredded cheese, divided

In a skillet over medium heat, cook turkey and onion in 1 tablespoon oil until meat is no longer pink; drain. Sprinkle with flour, chili powder, salt and pepper. Add water and bring to a boil. Reduce heat, cover and cook 8 to 10 minutes. In another skillet, fry tortillas in remaining oil about 20 seconds total, turning one time.

Preheat oven to 350°F. Cut 9 of the tortillas in half and place the cut edges of 1 tortilla against the short side of a greased 9 x 13-inch baking dish. Overlap remaining tortilla halves until bottom of dish is covered. Spoon 2 cups meat mixture over tortillas and layer ½ cup salsa over meat. Sprinkle with ½ cup cheese. Repeat layers and top with remaining tortillas, meat sauce, salsa and cheese. Bake, uncovered, 20 minutes; sprinkle with remaining cheese. Bake 10 minutes more, or until cheese has melted.

Serves 4–6

Serve with Spanish rice.

Turkey Curry Blend

Everyone enjoys this savory pasta dish that is exotic enough to serve to company.

8 ounces processed cheese, cubed
1/2 cup water
2 cups cubed cooked turkey or chicken
1 (10-ounce) package frozen peas, thawed
1 teaspoon curry powder
3 cups curly pasta (fusilli, rotini, etc.)

Place cheese and water in a medium saucepan; cook over medium heat, stirring constantly, until cheese is melted and sauce is smooth. Stir in turkey, peas and curry powder; bring to a boil. Reduce heat and simmer, uncovered, 10 minutes. Meanwhile, cook pasta according to package directions; drain. Toss pasta with cheese mixture.

Serves 4

Serve with warm rolls and mango chutney.

Five-Can Chili

Although this tastes wonderful without any toppings, try a sprinkle of your favorite shredded cheese and a dollop of sour cream to really delight the taste buds.

2 (15-ounce) cans kidney beans, drained
1 (15-ounce) can chili beans in sauce
1 (15-ounce) can stewed diced tomatoes, drained
1 (15-ounce) can corn, drained

In a medium saucepan, combine all ingredients and simmer on low 30 minutes, covered. If using a slow cooker, combine all ingredients, and then cover and cook 4 to 6 hours on low.

Serves 4–6

Serve with warm cranberry muffins.

Corn Chip Casserole

No need to buy brand-name chips for this recipe—the house brands work just as well.

6 cups any-flavor corn chips, crushed fine
2 tablespoons grated onion
1 (10-ounce) can chili with beans
1 (10-ounce) can red enchilada sauce
1 (8-ounce) can tomato sauce
1½ cups shredded cheddar cheese

Topping:
1¼ cups sour cream or plain yogurt
2 cups flavored corn chips, crushed fine
½ cup shredded cheddar cheese

Preheat oven to 375°F. Measure 6 cups corn chips into a large mixing bowl. Add onion, chili, enchilada sauce, tomato sauce and 1½ cups cheddar cheese to chips. Stir to combine. Place mixture into a 9 x 9-inch baking dish and bake 20 minutes. Remove from oven and spread sour cream over the casserole. Top with 2 cups crushed corn chips and sprinkle with ½ cup cheese. Bake 5 to 8 minutes, until cheese is melted and bubbly.

Serves 4–6

Serve with a tossed green salad of spinach, red onions and your favorite dressing.

Spinach Casserole

Some people like to spice this dish up with a dash of hot sauce or a spoonful of salsa.

1 (10-ounce) package frozen chopped spinach, thawed and squeezed dry
2 eggs, beaten
1/2 cup milk
1/2 cup cubed processed cheese
1 tablespoon chopped onion
1/2 teaspoon salt
1 cup soft bread crumbs
4 1/2 teaspoons margarine, melted

Preheat oven to 350°F. In a large bowl, combine spinach, eggs, milk, cheese, onion and salt. Pour into a greased 1-quart baking dish. Combine bread crumbs and margarine, and sprinkle over top of mixture. Bake uncovered 30 minutes, or until a knife inserted in the center comes out clean.

Serves 4

Serve this with hot buttered biscuits and in-season fresh fruit.

> ***Recipe Tip:*** During the last few minutes of baking, add any of these crunchy toppers to give your dish a lift: chow mein noodles, crushed non-sugared cold cereal, crushed corn chips, crushed crackers, croutons, nuts, crushed pretzels or crushed tortilla chips.

Slow Cooker Red Beans and Rice

Check with the butcher for a ham bone. They're inexpensive and provide incredible flavor. Otherwise, use 1 cup cooked cubed ham.

**1 pound red kidney beans, soaked overnight
   in water, drained**
1 (14½-ounce) can stewed tomatoes
1 ham hock or ham bone
1 teaspoon dried basil leaf
1 teaspoon dried thyme
1 cup chopped onion
1 clove garlic, minced or 1 teaspoon garlic powder
Salt and pepper to taste
1½ cups cooked long-grain white rice

Cook beans in fresh water on stovetop 30 to 60 minutes, or until tender; drain. Put beans in slow cooker with stewed tomatoes, ham hock, basil, thyme, onion, garlic, salt and pepper. Cover and cook on low 6 hours. Remove ham hock and serve beans with hot cooked rice.

Serves 4–6.

Serve with cracked wheat rolls and stewed carrots.

Onion-Zucchini Bake

Top with leftover seasoned bread crumbs or finely crushed potato chips before baking to get a savory crunchy crust.

1 large onion, diced
3 cups thinly sliced zucchini
¼ cup margarine
2 eggs, beaten
¼ cup milk
½ teaspoon salt
¼ teaspoon pepper
1 tablespoon mustard
2 cups grated cheddar cheese, divided

Preheat oven to 375°F. Sauté onion and zucchini in margarine until tender. Place in shallow baking dish. Combine eggs, milk, salt, pepper, mustard and half the cheese. Pour over veggies and sprinkle the rest of the cheese on top. Bake 25 minutes, or until heated through.

Serves 4-6

Serve with brown rice or couscous.

Pasta with Clam Sauce

This sauce looks elegant and tastes like it came from a fancy restaurant. Next time, substitute the clams and clam juice with leftover diced chicken and ¼ cup water.

1 (8-ounce) can clams, chopped or minced, reserving clam juice
½ cup chopped onions
1 tablespoon parsley
2 tablespoons margarine
1 (10¾-ounce) can condensed cream of mushroom soup
¼ cup milk
1 to 2 tablespoons shredded Parmesan cheese
4 cups hot cooked linguini pasta

In a saucepan, cook clams, onion and parsley in margarine. Stir in soup, milk, clam juice and cheese. Cover and cook over low heat 10 minutes. Serve over cooked pasta.

Serves 4-6

Serve with a green salad of iceberg lettuce, sliced tomatoes and a creamy dressing.

Cyndi's Curried Coconut Chicken

Buy cans of coconut milk and curry powder packets at an ethnic food store for real discount prices.

1^1/$_2$ tablespoon vegetable oil
2 tablespoons curry powder
^{1}/$_2$ onion, thinly sliced
2 cloves garlic, crushed
2 cups diced cooked chicken
1 (14-ounce) can light coconut milk
1 (14.5-ounce) can stewed, diced tomatoes
1 (8-ounce) can tomato sauce
3 tablespoons sugar
1 teaspoon salt
1 teaspoon pepper

Heat oil and curry powder in a large skillet over medium-high heat 2 minutes. Stir in onions and garlic and cook 1 minute more. Add chicken, tossing lightly to coat with curry oil. Reduce heat to medium and simmer 7 to 10 minutes. Pour coconut milk, tomatoes, tomato sauce, sugar, salt and pepper into the pan, and stir to combine. Cover and simmer, stirring occasionally, approximately 30 minutes.

Serves 4

Serve with hot brown or white rice.

Chapter 7
Leftovers

With some common sense and creativity in the kitchen, you can use leftovers in such a way that they can be the foundation for a few more family meals each week.

The secret to using leftovers is not being afraid to add them to a recipe. If your recipe calls for chopped asparagus but you have a container of green beans in the refrigerator, substitute. When you come across a wonderful recipe for stir-fry beef, slice up the rest of the pork shoulder you served last night and substitute that in the mixture.

Think of it as creative cooking, and with good common sense, you can turn leftovers into something memorable.

Stuffed Potatoes and Stuffed Shells

When it comes to leftovers, having the right background food can make all the difference. With potatoes and jumbo pasta shells, it's hard to imagine anything inside that doesn't taste better when enclosed in these delicious casings. Keep a bag of potatoes and a box of jumbo pasta shells on hand at all times to deliver a variety of leftover mixtures to the dinner table.

Stuffed Potatoes

4 medium russet potatoes, baked and cooled
1 tablespoon margarine
1 teaspoon salt
1 tablespoon milk
2 to 3 cups leftover mixture of meat and vegetables
1 cup shredded cheese, your choice

Preheat oven to 350°F. Slice potatoes in half lengthwise and carefully scoop out insides. Be careful to leave a ¼-inch-thick potato "bowl." Place insides in a medium-size bowl. Add margarine, salt and milk, and mix thoroughly until potatoes are smooth. Fold in leftover mixture until well blended. Carefully spoon potato mixture back into the potato-skin bowls and place filled potatoes in a baking dish. Top with cheese and bake, uncovered, 25 minutes, or until heated through.

Serves 4 (2 potato halves each)

Stuffed Shells

1 (12-ounce) box jumbo shells, uncooked
1 (16-ounce) jar Alfredo or spaghetti sauce, divided
2 to 3 cups leftover mixture of meat and vegetables
¼ cup Parmesan cheese

Cook shells according to package directions. When tender, set shells on wax paper until cool, making sure they don't touch each other. Meanwhile, spread 1 cup sauce on the bottom of a greased 9 x 13-inch baking dish. When shells are cool enough to handle, spoon leftover mixture into shells. Place open-side down in baking dish and cover shells with remaining sauce. Top with cheese and cover with foil. Bake 30 minutes, or until hot and bubbling.

Serves 4 (2 shells each)

As long as the mixture consistency is similar to sloppy joes, some fantastic leftover mixtures that work well with stuffed potatoes and stuffed shells are:
  » Sloppy Joe meat
  » Taco meat
  » Shredded chicken, pork or beef
  » Chopped cooked broccoli
  » Vegetable medley
  » Leftover vegetable stew, drained of broth
  » Leftover cooked beans and rice
  » Cooked spinach and onions
  » Cooked Italian sausage

Basic Crêpes

Contrary to everything you've heard about French cuisine, crêpes are really easy to make—simply mix a few inexpensive ingredients and cook. Soon you'll have delicate little pancakes just ready to wrap around your leftover mixtures. Crêpes can be made in advance, then layered with wax paper and wrapped in foil or plastic, and refrigerated for up to 3 days. Let crêpes warm to room temperature before serving.

3 eggs
⅛ teaspoon salt
1½ cups flour
1½ cups milk
2 tablespoons vegetable oil

In a medium bowl, combine eggs and salt; add flour alternately with milk. Beat after each addition until smooth. Add oil and beat, and then refrigerate at least 1 hour. Take 2 tablespoons batter and pour into a 6-inch nonstick skillet over medium heat. Turn the skillet to spread the batter into a thin layer at the bottom of the skillet. Cook until bottom is brown, and then turn crêpe to brown the other side (about 1 minute).

Enhanced savory: Add ¼ teaspoon salt and ¼ cup chopped fresh herbs, spinach or sun-dried tomatoes to the egg mixture.

Enhanced sweet: Add 2 tablespoons sugar and 1 teaspoon vanilla to the egg mixture.

Makes 12 crêpes

There are many ways to incorporate leftovers into crêpes:
- » Ham, Swiss cheese, scrambled egg
- » Onions, tomato and cheese
- » Shredded chicken and sautéed bell peppers
- » Shredded beef, mushrooms and sour cream
- » Mushrooms, tomato, spinach and onions
- » Zucchini, onions, crumbled bacon and cheese

Quiche

A rich savory custard pie, quiche has evolved into a meal that is perfect for breakfast, lunch or dinner. Just right for families on the go, quiche can easily handle a variety of leftover meats and veggies, or it's great on its own as a hearty meal. This French egg pie is easy to make and is sure to please.

Frozen pastry for single-crust pie shell, thawed
8 slices bacon
1 medium onion, thinly sliced
4 eggs, beaten
1 cup half-and-half
1 cup milk
¼ teaspoon salt
1 tablespoon flour
1½ cups shredded Swiss cheese

Preheat oven to 450°F. Place shell in pie pan, cover with foil and bake 6 minutes. Remove foil and bake an additional 5 minutes, or until pastry is dry. Remove pie shell from oven and set aside. Reduce oven temperature to 325°F.

Meanwhile, in a large skillet, cook bacon until crisp. Drain and reserve 1 tablespoon of drippings. Crumble bacon and set aside. Cook onion slices in bacon drippings until tender; drain. In a medium-size bowl, stir in eggs, half-and-half, milk and salt. Stir in bacon and onion. Toss flour and cheese together; add to egg mixture. Pour egg mixture into hot pie crust and bake, uncovered, 50 minutes, or until a knife inserted in the center comes out clean. Let stand 10 minutes before serving.

Serves 4-6

Quiche is a vehicle for just about any meat and veggie combination. Just make sure the additions are dry:

» Cooked pork sausage and mushrooms
» Cubed ham and chopped spinach and broccoli mixed
» Diced potato and onion
» Shredded zucchini and chopped tomato
» Corn and cooked spinach
» Canadian bacon and cheese

Homemade Soup

Soup is the perfect vehicle for leftovers, no matter how much or little there is. When you start with a basic soup base, the possibilities are endless. You may never be able to make the same recipe twice, as your leftovers will change from week to week. Serve with crusty rolls and each new creation is nourishing and hearty.

Buy broth if it's on sale or try making your own broth for a great way to save money. Save chicken bones in the refrigerator and make up some broth on a slow evening. Just dump the chicken bones in a saucepan and cover with water. Simmer on low about 2 hours, skim the fat off and either store it in the refrigerator or freeze it. The same thing works for the water you cook vegetables in. Keep a jar in the refrigerator that you can pour the vegetable water in. When it's full, it's time for soup.

Broth Soup Starter
3¹/₂ cups water or broth (made from scratch or using bouillon)
¹/₂ cup chopped onion
¹/₂ teaspoon dried oregano
¹/₂ teaspoon garlic salt
¹/₄ teaspoon pepper
Add in meat and veggies as desired

Combine all ingredients in a slow cooker and cook on low 6 hours. On the stovetop, combine all ingredients in a saucepan and cook covered on medium-low 1 hour.

Try a few of these mix 'n' match ingredients with the basic soup starter.
» 1 (10-ounce) can beans, your choice
» 2 cups cubed cooked chicken or turkey

- » 2 cups browned and drained ground beef or sausage
- » 1 cup chopped celery
- » 1 cup loosely packed frozen mixed vegetables
- » 3 potatoes, peeled and cubed
- » 1 (16-ounce) can diced tomatoes, drained
- » 3 cups any combination: sliced celery, carrots, parsnips, mushrooms, broccoli, cauliflower, corn or green beans
- » 2 cups shredded cabbage
- » 3 cups hot cooked noodles
- » 3 cups hot cooked rice
- » 1 tablespoon Worcestershire sauce

Serves 4–6

Cream Soup Starter
2 cups powdered nonfat milk
³/₄ cup cornstarch
¹/₄ cup powdered instant chicken bouillon
2 tablespoons dried onion flakes
1 teaspoon dried basil leaves
1 teaspoon thyme
¹/₂ teaspoon pepper

Combine all ingredients and mix well. Store in an airtight container. Equals 9 cans of soup. To start a cream soup for 4 servings, use 1⅓ cups dry Cream Soup Starter and 5 cups water.

Combine ingredients in a saucepan over medium heat, stir and cook until thickened. Add other ingredients as desired and simmer until heated through. Add water as needed if soup becomes too thick.

Try a few of these mix 'n' match ingredients with the
Cream Soup Starter:
- » 2 cups cubed cooked chicken or turkey
- » 2 cups browned and drained sausage
- » 2 cups ham, diced
- » 1 cup loosely packed frozen mixed vegetables
- » 3 cups cooked potato cubes
- » 3 cups any combination: carrots, parsnips, mush-rooms, broccoli, cauliflower, corn or green beans.
- » 1 (6½-ounce) can clams, drained
- » ¼ cup chopped bell peppers, red or green
- » 1 celery stalk, diced

Serves 4–6

Stuffed Muffins

Make a batch of cornbread muffins according to the package directions; however, don't fill the muffin cups quite so full—just about halfway will do. Then, place a heaping spoonful of leftover mix in the center of each one and bake, again according to the package directions. The muffin batter rises up around the mixture, making a fun and surprising side that complements any main course. The flavor combinations are endless—it just depends on what's in the refrigerator.

Try these delicious add-ins:
- » Leftover chili will complement a Mexi-style meal.
- » Hamburger and a little shredded cheese plus a squirt of ketchup make a cheeseburger muffin.
- » Chicken, crumbled bacon and a dollop of ranch dressing deliver a fresh chicken ranch flavor.
- » Vegetable blend (such as peas, carrots and corn) topped with cheese is a nice vegetable alternative.

Serves 4–6

Hot Cups

House-brand refrigerated biscuits are the perfect container for a tasty center of your choosing. These can star as a main dish or complement an entree as a unique side dish.

1 package of 6-count refrigerated biscuits
6 (6-ounce) custard cups
Filling of your choice

Preheat oven to 400°F. Open a biscuit tube and separate biscuits. Grease the outside of custard cups, and then press one biscuit over the bottom and halfway down the side of each custard cup. Place cups, dough side up, on a baking sheet and bake 7 minutes or until lightly browned. Immediately remove biscuits from cups and place upright on the baking sheet.

Meanwhile, prepare a filling mixture and spoon into biscuit cups. Return to oven and bake 7 to 10 minutes, or until heated through.

Serves 4–6

Try these tasty filler ideas or create your own:
» 2 (6-ounce) cans tuna, well drained; ⅓ cup mayonnaise; 1 cup cooked peas; and tomato slices and cheese to top biscuit cups
» 3 cups taco-seasoned ground beef; 1 (10-ounce) cup kidney beans, drained; and 3 cups shredded cheese, your choice

» 2 cups cooked chicken cubed; ½ cup Alfredo sauce; ½ cup frozen mixed vegetables, thawed; and crumbled butter crackers for topping
» 3 cups vegetable blend; ½ cup plain yogurt; 1 teaspoon mustard; and Parmesan cheese for topping

Leftovers

Stir-fry

Anything and everything can go into a stir-fry, from
bits of leftover cooked beef to shredded chicken, and
just about any vegetable combination imaginable. As
long as you have a few solid ingredients on hand at all
times, you can have a stir-fry meal once a week to use
up any lingering leftovers.

3 tablespoons margarine
2 cups cubed or shredded leftover meat (such as steak,
    roast beef, shrimp, chicken, turkey or pork)
1 (20-ounce) can pineapple chunks, drained
    reserving syrup
1 tablespoon vinegar
2 tablespoons soy sauce
1 tablespoon sugar
¼ teaspoon salt
2 tablespoons cornstarch
2 tablespoons water
1 to 2 cups vegetable blend or frozen Oriental vegetable
    mix, thawed
4 cups hot cooked rice

Melt margarine in a medium skillet over medium-
high heat. Add meat and stir occasionally 3 minutes.
Add enough water to the pineapple syrup to measure
2¼ cups. Stir pineapple liquid, vinegar, soy sauce,
sugar and salt into skillet and simmer 4 minutes. Mix
cornstarch and water, and gradually stir into meat
mixture. Cook, stirring constantly, until mixture
thickens and bubbles. Stir in pineapple chunks and
vegetables, and cook until crisp-tender, about 3 minutes. Serve over hot cooked rice.

Serves 4

Here are some excellent stir-fry ingredients:

» 1 cup sliced celery
» 1 cup frozen or canned peas
» 1 cup frozen or canned corn
» 1 cup frozen or canned green beans
» ½ cup mushroom pieces and stems
» ½ cup chopped onion
» 1 cup chow mein noodles, added with the vegetables
» 1 cup cubed squash
» ½ cup chopped green or red bell pepper
» ½ cup sliced water chestnuts
» 1 cup cooked orzo pasta
» ¼ cup coarsely crushed peanuts

Pot Pies

Pot pies are the ultimate leftovers vehicle—a piping hot combo of cooked vegetables, creamy gravy and tender meats. With a crispy topping of pie crust or dough, a pot pie is a surprise dinner, as you never know what you'll get when you break through that first warm flaky layer. Usually pot pies are baked in a casserole dish with a bread covering on top, and the secret to a successful pot pie is the crust. Here are three crust variations to top off any blend of leftover mixture.

Cornbread Crust
1 (6-ounce) box cornbread mix
1/3 cup milk
2 tablespoons margarine, melted
1 egg
1/4 cup shredded Parmesan cheese
4 to 6 cups meat and vegetable mixture

Preheat oven to 400°F. In a medium bowl, lightly blend cornbread mix, milk, melted margarine, egg and cheese. Place meat mixture into a greased 9 x 13-inch baking dish. Drop cornbread mixture by spoonfuls over the top and smooth to cover completely. Bake 20 minutes, or until cornbread is golden brown and mixture is bubbling.

Serves 4-6

Traditional Crust
1 (9-inch) frozen pastry pie crust, thawed
4 to 6 cups meat and vegetable mixture

Preheat oven to 425°F. Spoon meat mixture into a greased round 9-inch glass pie dish. Top with pastry,

and then seal and flute edges. Cut 4 small slits in top crust for venting. Bake 30 minutes until crust is deep golden brown. Let stand 15 minutes before serving.

Serves 4–6

Refrigerated Biscuit Crust
4 to 6 cups meat and vegetable mixture
1 (10-count) can refrigerated biscuit dough
2 tablespoons shredded Parmesan cheese
¼ teaspoon pepper

Preheat oven to 400°F. Pour meat mixture into 1½-quart baking dish. Top with biscuits and sprinkle with Parmesan cheese and pepper. Bake 15 to 18 minutes, or until biscuits are deep golden brown.

Serves 4–6

Winning pot pie fillings—just mix and pour into greased baking dishes:

» 2 cups cubed cooked turkey breast; 1 (16-ounce) package frozen veggies; and 1 (12-ounce) jar turkey gravy

» ½ pound browned ground beef; 1 (16-ounce) can pork and beans; 1 stalk sliced green celery; ½ onion, diced; and ½ green bell pepper, diced

» ½ pound browned ground beef; 1 cup chopped mushrooms; 1 (10¾-ounce) can condensed cream of mushroom soup; and 1 (9-ounce) package frozen corn, thawed

» 2 cups cooked shredded chicken; 1 (16-ounce) jar Alfredo pasta sauce; ½ cup milk; 1 (16-ounce) package frozen mixed vegetables, thawed and drained; and ¼ cup Parmesan cheese

Leftovers

» 2 cups cooked diced chicken; 1 (8-ounce) package cream cheese, softened; 1 (4-ounce) can chopped green chilies, well drained; ⅓ cup enchilada sauce; and ¼ cup grated Parmesan cheese
» 1 red bell pepper, chopped; 1 (16-ounce) package frozen mixed vegetables, thawed and drained; 1½ cups shredded peeled potatoes; 1 (1½-ounce) package white sauce mix; 2 cups milk; ¼ teaspoon pepper; and 1½ cups shredded cheddar cheese

Notes

Notes

Notes

Notes

Notes

Notes

Index

buying, 21
Cheater Potato Soup, 40
Corn Chowder, 38
Ham and Cheese Potatoes,
    107
Slow Cooker Red Beans and
    Rice, 129
Stovetop Han and Potatoes,
    103
Hearty Orzo Chowder, 44
Homemade Soup, 140–42
Hot Cups, 144–45

I

impulse buying, 18
Italian Mac Recipe, 86

L

Lasagna, Vegetable, 73
lists, grocery, 3–6
loss leaders, 3

M

Macaroni and cheese, boxed
    Chili Macaroni Soup, 38
    Italian Mac Recipe, 86
Mandarin Couscous Salad,
    46
Manicotti, Turkey, 121
marinades, using, 20
meat, poultry, and fish: buying,
    20–24
Meat Loaf, Budget, 92
Melon Boats, 59
milk, buying, 25
Muffins, Stuffed, 143

N

Noodle Rice Pilaf, 75
nutrition, 32

O

Onion-Zucchini Bake, 130
Orange Pork Chops and Rice,
    106
outlet stores, for bakeries, 23,
    28

P

Pancake with Sausage, Puffed,
    114
pantry, items for, 36
Parmesan-Crusted Potatoes, 54
pasta
    buying, 24
    Pasta with Clam Sauce, 131
    Stuffed Potatoes and Stuffed
        Shells, 134–35
    Vegetable Lasagna, 73
Peanut Sauce, Spicy, 105
Pilaf, Noodle Rice, 75
planning, 2
Polenta, Baked, 74
pork
    Budget Meat Loaf, 92
    buying, 21–22
    Curry Pork with Apples, 108
    Pork Loaves, 109
    Pork Stir-Fry with Spicy
        Peanut Sauce, 105
    Orange Pork Chops and
        Rice, 106
    Stuffed Pork Chops, 110
Potato chips, 34

potatoes
All in One Dish, 89
Autumn Stew, 45
Bean and Ham Soup, 42
Cheater Potato Soup, 40
Confetti Hash, 119
Farmer's Strata, 91
Fish Stick Casserole, 99
Ham and Cheese Potatoes, 107
Parmesan-Crusted Potatoes, 54
Potatoes and Peas, 70
Roasted Red Potatoes, 64
Scalloped Potatoes, 63
Slow Cooker Pot Roast with Vegetables, 118
Stovetop Ham and Potatoes, 103
Stuffed Potatoes and Stuffed Shells, 134
Turkey Shepherd's Pie, 122
pot pies, options for, 148–50
price comparison, 7–8
price guide, 10–14
price matching, 6–7
produce, 18–20
product placement and appearance, 17
Puffed Pancake with Sausage, 114

reduced-sale meats, 22
rice
Curried Pork with Apples, 108
Ground Beef and Rice, 90
in casseroles and soups, 39
Mexican Haystacks, 93
Noodle Rice Pilaf, 75
Orange Pork Chops and Rice, 106
Slow Cooker Red Beans and Rice, 129
Roasted Red Potatoes, 64

S
salads
Asian, 48
Cucumber, 52
Easy Fruit, 51
Egg, 50
Mandarin Couscous, 46
Taco Pasta, 47
sales, 2–3
Saucy Steak, 117
sausage
Bean Barley Soup, 41
Breakfast Casserole, 113
Puffed Pancake with Sausage, 114
Spaghetti Pie, 112
Ziti and Sausage, 111
Zucchini Boats, 66
Scalloped Potatoes, 63
seasonal shopping, 19
shopping tips, 16–18
slow cooker
cooking with, 20

Z

Ziti and Sausage, 111
zucchini
Onion–Zucchini Bake, 130
Zucchini Boats, 66
Zucchini Cakes, 55

Metric Conversion Chart

Liquid and Dry Measures

U.S.	Canadian	Australian
¼ teaspoon	1 mL	1 ml
½ teaspoon	2 mL	2 ml
1 teaspoon	5 mL	5 ml
1 tablespoon	15 mL	20 ml
¼ cup	50 mL	60 ml
⅓ cup	75 mL	80 ml
½ cup	125 mL	125 ml
⅔ cup	150 mL	170 ml
¾ cup	175 mL	190 ml
1 cup	250 mL	250 ml
1 quart	1 liter	1 litre

Temperature Conversion Chart

Fahrenheit	Celsius
250	120
275	140
300	150
325	160
350	180
375	190
400	200
425	220
450	230
475	240
500	260

Jennifer Maughan is a freelance writer and editor with more than 15 years of experience in the publishing industry. Her areas of specialty include travel, food, celebrations, parenting and family life. When she's not working, Jennifer enjoys spending time with her husband and three children, whether it's gardening, biking, or traveling.